'Can you hear me, mother?'

'Can you hear me, mother?' SANDY POWELL'S *lifetime of* Music-Hall

Sandy Powell's
story told to
Harry Stanley

JUPITER BOOKS

First published in 1975 by
Jupiter Books (London) Limited
167 Hermitage Road, London N4.

SBN 904041 387

Copyright © Harry Stanley 1975

Set in 11/12pt Monotype Imprint 101 by
The Lancashire Typesetting Company Limited, Bolton.
Printed and bound in Great Britain.

Contents

ACKNOWLEDGEMENTS

THE AUTHOR wishes to thank the following for their great help in the preparation of this book: Sandy Powell M.B.E., a wonderful, kind and modest man without whose complete co-operation through countless hours the present work would never have been completed. His lovely wife, Kay, whose intimate knowledge and experience of the theatre was most helpful, and also Kay's sister, Ida White, for much valuable family and theatrical information.

Additionally thanks must go to Eric Redfern, editor of the *Eastbourne Gazette and Herald*; Norman Meadows; Alf Lake and Alf Cozens for their personal memories of 'Mr Eastbourne'; Michael Pointon; Malcolm Nash; Barry Simons, a great authority on pantomine; G. Headland; Arthur Lane; Bunny Baron; Harry Lester and Roy Jeffries for photographs, bills and recollections of their happy association with Sandy; Jack Johns, a retired headmaster whose neighbourly wielding of colons, commas and full points was greatly appreciated (if not always understood); and, Mick Canning for taking the photographs used on the jacket.

Thanks also go to my wife, Rita, whose enjoyment of her favourite TV and radio programmes was constantly interrupted by my typewriter, yet she never complained (well, not much). And to John Maxwell and Roy Bloom who gave me encouragement and consideration through all stages of publication, as did the indefatigable Anthony Frewin.

Finally, I would like to thank you, dear Reader, for having bought, begged or borrowed this book and hope that you enjoy reading about a very special person as much as I did writing about him. A star who continues to remind us of the glories of *live, professional* entertainment at a time when we seem set to drown in a sea of electronic gallimaufry and the hollow trumpetings of Promotion.

Draw back the curtain and on with the show!

HARRY STANLEY
Pevensey Bay, 1975.

I

Early Doors

THE place was the Opera House in Cape Town, South Africa, the date was 30th January 1975, and the show was *The Golden Years of Music Hall*.

The star of the show, which was on a five months' tour of Central and Southern Africa, was Sandy Powell. This was his seventy-fifth birthday and far away from his birthplace in Yorkshire he was still working almost seventy years after making his first stage appearance.

Sandy can claim to have had a theatrical background: his mother, Lily, was a trouper who worked in the small theatres in the north of England during the eighteen nineties. Lily was introduced into 'the business' by her sister who, with her husband, did a double act. It was their help and encouragement that enabled her to make the best use of her strong natural voice, to step-dance and to develop her obvious flair for comedy. Lily was quick and eager to learn and her talents were soon moulded to form a song-and-dance act which was launched under the glamorous name of 'Lily Le Main'.

The grim industrial areas of the North offered very little to the young people; their only means of livelihood was the hard and unpleasant work in the mills or mines. In this environment the stage was an escape; it gave one the chance to travel, see new places, and there was always the hope of fame and fortune.

It was arranged that Lily would work on the same bill as her sister which meant that they were able to travel together and stay in the same digs. Lily now had opportunities of professional help and advice and she was encouraged to watch other acts working on the bill. She acquired a set of marionette figures and presented them as a separate act: 'Lillette's Living Marionettes'.

Lily was eighteen when she met and fell in love with a handsome young stage hand named Powell. After a lightning courtship they married and moved into a small one-up-one-down terrace house in Russoms Yard, Bridgegate, Rotherham. A year later on the 30th January 1900 their son was born and christened Albert Arthur Powell. His proud father gave his red-headed son the nickname 'Sandy'.

Lily, now having a child to care for, had to give up stage work. Her husband had a day-time job as well as working at nights in the theatre, but the small amount he earned and his fondness for drink made his support of the domestic economy quite inadequate. The young girls in the theatre caught his roving eye and this hardly helped matters. There were the inevitable quarrels which became more frequent and bitter as time went on. When Sandy was about four years old his father left home and never returned.

Lily now had all the responsibility of bringing up her child, but she wasted little time feeling sorry for herself. She found a job at a nearby public house as a waitress who also entertained the customers by singing and getting them to join in the choruses. A customer with the prospect of free beer would often accompany her on a tinny-sounding piano. Lily with her professional experience became very popular with the patrons and her wages augmented by their tips made it possible to have Sandy well looked after during her working hours.

Some weeks later Lily was offered another job as the resident singer at The White Lion, a large hostelry in Doncaster. She was now a featured artist and therefore no longer had to serve at tables. At weekends and on special nights she did comedy gags as well as singing. She also introduced the guest artist, who was usually a popular local male singer. Requests from customers for her to sing their favourite numbers resulted in more generous tipping. This provided the extra money needed to obtain a room nearby so that Sandy could live with her in Doncaster.

Sandy was far too young to be allowed on licenced premises and the problem of having him looked after while Lily was working became urgent. It was solved by hiding him behind the piano in the corner of the large bar room. Of course Sandy thought it was great fun to be in this secret hideout, especially since he was frequently and surreptitiously supplied with biscuits and lemonade.

Lily was now anxious to get back to the stage and when she was not working she used her time to rehearse and polish her original act. She also planned and worked on two new ones to be known as 'Serio-Comic' and 'Living Marionettes'. Having three different acts, Lily contacted agents to inform them that she was available for bookings.

Quite a number of dates came in and Sandy had his first experience of touring which was to him a great adventure and even more exciting when it involved a train journey.

He was fascinated by the marionette figures and played with them every day with the exception of Sunday, when they had to be packed in a basket and put in the care of the railway guard. On arrival at their destination the basket was left in the luggage office while they looked around for the cheapest digs available.

On Monday at the theatre the dolls were carefully unpacked and Sandy helped his mother set them up for her act. Every night he stood in the wings to watch, completely fascinated and absorbed in the way she brought them to life on the stage.

Lily soon became aware of his great interest in the dolls and taught him how to handle them. It didn't take him long to become quite expert in their manipulation, so much so that Lily put him into the act. While still in his fifth year Sandy actually worked on the stage manipulating a marionette figure, putting his head through the curtain on to the shoulders of the doll and bringing it to life by his skilful handling.

Life at this time was certainly not a bed of roses; there were hard times and these were too frequent to ensure a stable and secure living, but Lily saw that Sandy didn't suffer and that despite adverse circumstances he would have enough to eat and be decently clothed. Mornings were spent at the theatre where she taught him some elementary dance steps and movements, and encouraged him to watch the speciality acts rehearsing – specially the acrobats and jugglers. The children of these artists often took part and even the youngest were taught the skills of their parents. Becoming friends with these children gave Sandy the opportunity to learn some of their tricks, and very soon he was able to juggle competently with a few small objects.

Eventually Lily and Sandy ran into a bad patch and after a period of hardship and disillusionment she managed to fix up a tour of small variety theatres in and around Manchester.

It was in Manchester that Sandy made his debut as a chorus singer. He was planted in the gallery with the rest of the audience who were quite unaware of his connection with the act on stage. His part was to join in the choruses of Lily's songs and this he did by singing as loudly as he could. Lily hearing the voice from the 'top shelf' would look up, make a gesture to the audience to stop singing, and make signs to Sandy to stand up and continue to sing. His first attempt, however, was a disaster. Being nervous he came in too early and had his face slapped by an irate lady sitting near by who told him in no uncertain terms to 'Shut up!' She obviously regarded him as a cheeky young brat who was out to spoil the show. Despite the extreme embarrassment of his first public performance, he gradually learnt the correct timing and the audience loved his clear soprano voice.

During this period in Manchester Sandy had his first chance of seeing some of the big-time stars. The Palace, Hippodrome, and the Empire at Ardwick Green were large and beautiful theatres, where for a few coppers he could climb up the steep winding stairs to the gallery. It was from this high viewpoint that he looked down on the stars of the Music Hall: Harry Weldon, George Formby Snr, Wilkie Bard and Harry Lauder – but his particular idol was Harry Weldon.

Harry Weldon must be numbered among the all-time greats. He was a master of burlesque, a droll character of the type now referred to as the 'anti-hero'. His most famous role was that of 'Stiffy' the goalkeeper in the 'Fred Karno Football Sketch'. He would lean dolefully against the goalpost bored with the inactivity, trying to fold his arms which kept slipping through each other. Then there would be a flurry of excitement caused by an impending attack and this would be followed by another period of

*Lilette, Sandy's mother, when she presented 'Lilette's Living Marionettes'.
Circa 1895.*

tedium when he tried to put his hands into his pockets only to find that his shorts had no pockets. It was a classic example of superbly timed mime. Great comedy also came from his exchanges with the villain of the piece who tried to bribe him to lose the game. (In the original sketch the part of the villain was played by Charlie Chaplin.) The odd mannerisms of Harry Weldon, such as a peculiar whistle while he talked, and a catch phrase ' 's no use' made a never-to-be-forgotten impression on young Sandy, who later imitated the style of this great artist.

One of Sandy's most vivid boyhood memories was when he was about ten years old, and saw his idol standing on the platform at Victoria Station in Leeds. He shouted excitedly to his mother, 'I must speak to him.' Lily replied, 'He wont bite you, why dont you go over and speak to him?' 'But what can I say to him?' queried Sandy. 'Why not ask him the time?' said Lily. Plucking up courage Sandy nervously approached the great man and said 'Excuse me sir, will you please tell me the time?' Mr Weldon obliged and Sandy's day was well and truly made. This was the first and only time he ever spoke to his idol, though some years later he had the great thrill of actually deputising for Harry Weldon.

Sandy's first visible appearance on the stage came around this time when Lily worked the Hippodrome, Keighley. On the same bill was the great Dr Walford Bodie, described as 'Mesmerist and Electrical Wizard'. Bodie was one of the biggest draw-cards of the day. He was an extraordinary man who claimed to alleviate suffering by the use of electricity and mesmerism. Cripples were brought to him in the hope of a cure, and often sticks and crutches were displayed in front of the theatre as proof of his remarkable 'cures'. His use of the title 'Doctor' was vigorously disclaimed in his many clashes with the medical profession, as was the use of the medical qualification M.D. after his name. When challenged Bodie blandly replied that it stood for 'Merry Devil'. He was undoubtedly a charlatan, but believed his own patter, and without question was a great showman. His name on the bill broke box-office records. In his act Dr Bodie called for members of the public to come up on the stage to assist him in some of his amazing experiments. He used many 'stooges', confederates who sat in the audience as ordinary members of the public and would immediately respond to his appeal for volunteers. They had received their instructions backstage prior to the performance. Sandy was asked to 'volunteer' and his contribution was to work the 'Electric Chair' gag. He sat in the audience and when volunteers were asked for, he joined in the rush for the stage. He was then invited to sit on a chair placed 'accidently' near the footlights. Bodie, a most imposing figure with waxed moustache and piercing eyes made hypnotic passes and apparently put Sandy into a trance. A few moments later Bodie pointed dramatically in his direction, whereupon Sandy jumped sharply upwards as though he had received an electric shock. Sandy would look very suspiciously at the chair and then the Wizard would lift it up to show that it was harmless and free of trickery. Sandy would be invited to sit down again. The episode was repeated and used as a running gag which ended with Sandy rushing off stage and presumably out of the theatre. By the end of the week Sandy had become quite expert as a stooge, and was rewarded by a gracious pat on the head by the doctor who also slipped a few coppers into his hand. They worked with the good doctor quite a few times after that, and each time Sandy was among the first of the volunteers.

At the age of nine years Sandy made his first solo appearance on the stage as a 'Boy Soprano'. At that time children were not allowed to perform in public under the age of eleven years. A certain amount of subterfuge was called for and although he was a sturdy lad, and when dressed up could pass muster, the birth certificate of his cousin Billy was borrowed in order to get a licence to work in theatres.

Sandy was now booked as a separate act on the same bill as his mother – Lily Le Main. Very much against his will, he was forced to wear what seemed to him a most unmanly velvet suit with lace collar. His function was to sing in competition with the din set up by the late arrivals. The ballad 'Sweet Sixteen' was the very first song he sang, the first line of which 'I love you as I never loved before', was a fitting introduction to his first audience as a soloist. This ballad, together with 'Love's Old Sweet Song' was the only ammunition which he had to quell these tardy scufflings. He felt a little disappointed that he was put on to sing when there was a lot of noise going on at the same time. He didn't realise at the time that it was good training for him. When he finished his act, he helped behind the scenes setting up the marionettes and later did his little piece in his mother's act before changing back into his velvet suit ready for the second house.

They worked some strange places; there were small mining towns where matinées were given in the morning and the front seats looked as if they were occupied by black-faced comics. The miners, who had come straight from their night shift, would sit there with their lanterns and were usually appreciative of Sandy's singing. When they went over the border into Scotland, Lily dressed Sandy in a Scottish outfit and he sang Harry Lauder songs, such as 'I love a Lassie' and 'Roaming In The Gloaming'. This idea of matching songs with the clothes to suit the localities where they worked was quite successful. When they worked the mining areas Sandy was dressed and billed as 'The Singing Pit Lad', carried a miner's lamp and sang songs about the perils of working down a mine. In time his sweet high voice began to fade, and although he received a lot of sympathy when he started to croak 'Don't Go Down in the Mine Daddy', there was a limit to which the indulgence of those mining-district audiences would go, and it was realised that his vocal career was finished.

Making their way back to Rotherham, Lily started to look around for the next thing to do. She realised that young Sandy had potential, he was keen and had a great aptitude for the stage. About this time cinemas were beginning to gain in popularity and in addition to the silent films they used two or three variety acts. The cinema proprietors did not really want the acts, but had to have something to fill in the breaks caused by having to change the film reels. The projector also needed the time to cool down. In the trade these variety acts were known as 'Lantern Coolers'. The cinemas were pretty primitive places and more often than not derelict factories, old churches or mission halls. The seating consisted of long continuous rows of wooden forms and the cost of admission was two pence. One of these cinemas was quite near home and this gave Lily an idea which the management liked very much. Slides were made on which the words of popular chorus songs were printed. Lily sang the songs and the audience joined in the choruses from the words projected on to the screen. Sandy was given the job of feeding the slides into the house magic lantern and so earned his keep. The venture was a great success and with constant changes of programme, it meant work for many weeks. The money wasn't very good, but as they were home with no fares to pay they were not too badly off. Sandy did not waste his time and rehearsed lengthily on a new solo act. By watching other acts, he had picked up and remembered much of the patter and stories. He selected those he thought best suited him, and with his mother's help knocked them together into a routine. He could also do impressions of his favourites such as Harry Weldon, Wilkie Bard, George Formby Snr and Harry Lauder. Lily also helped him to work out a tap-dance routine – a kind of Lancashire clog dance.

Because of travelling around Sandy had very little in the way of conventional education, and although officially he had to attend a school in each town he worked, for one reason or another he had not done so. All in all, his formal schooling probably amounted to not more than six months. All that he remembers of his very limited school days was the children making fun of him because of his red hair, and that when teacher found out that he was on the stage he was made to sing. It was Lily who taught him to read and write and the remainder of his education came from life experience. As it was, he was left much to himself and developed his own natural style.

When the cinema engagement came to an end Lily went back to working her regular act and they went off on a tour of small theatres and cinemas in the North-East. One night, while Lily was on stage at the Globe Cinema at Gosforth, near Newcastle-on-Tyne, Sandy was backstage showing his talent for the benefit of the stagehands, mainly impressions of popular stars. Unbeknown to Sandy the manager was watching him, and when Lily came off stage he asked her why her lad wasn't working that week. Lily replied that Sandy's voice had broken and so he had to give up singing. 'That shouldn't stop him,' said the manager, 'he does some good impressions of Weldon, Wilkie Bard, Lauder and George Formby and he could do a nice little act.' He told Lily that the Rawes & Clarence Agency was auditioning at the nearby Benwell Cinema and suggested that Sandy should have a try since he stood a good chance. Sandy gave the audition and his act impressed Mr Arthur Clarence sufficiently to book him for a juvenile revue they were putting on the road. Mr Clarence was a helpful man and he gave Sandy some good advice. 'Have you a special favourite among the big stars, son?' he asked. 'Harry Weldon' was the instant reply.

'Right!' said Mr Clarence 'Model yourself on him. When you rehearse keep thinking all the time "I'm Harry Weldon". Act like him, work like him and it will give you a start, and then later on you can develop your own style.' Taking Mr Clarence literally, Sandy 'borrowed' Harry Weldon's act completely. In all innocence he thought that Mr Weldon would be pleased if he ever heard about his youthful imitator.

The juvenile Revue was called *Autumn* and Sandy was the only boy in the company, which included a troup of ten young girls. *Autumn* opened at the Empire, Easington Colliery in County Durham, and was quite success-ful during its tour of the small towns in the North-East. Excitement was great when the cast were told that shortly they were going to work at the Palace, Sunderland. In those days it was considered the absolute 'tops' to work there. Sandy thought that it would be a chance for him to be seen by a big agent who would bound to be impressed by his versatility. In the show he had many roles: as red-nosed comic, impressionist, juggler and acrobat.

Alas, a week before the date at the Palace, he received a letter from the agency informing him that the show was being 're-arranged' and that his services as a performer were no longer required, but he was wanted to take charge of the baggage. Sandy was absolutely shattered and politely told them what they could do as far as the job of baggage-boy was concerned.

Lily, a shrewd business woman and ever mindful of Sandy's ambitions, felt that it would be a good time to launch out with their own juvenile revue. Sandy was installed as the principal comedian, doing impressions, cracking gags and telling jokes, which were all filched from the best star acts. He was supported by a troupe of six young girls and four boys who did concerted singing and dancing, such as the Highland Fling, and reels in a scene which included Sandy appearing as 'The Ideal Scotch Comedian'. He now blushes every time he thinks of it, for at the time Harry Lauder was at the peak of his popularity.

The revue was called *Are We All Here?* which was the title of a popular song of the day. The wage given to each performer was twelve shillings and sixpence a week, Lily being responsible for their food and housing. The entire company stayed in the same digs – the cheapest that could be found. The task of feeding a bunch of hungry youngsters was quite a problem; it could certainly be costly, so each day started with a hefty breakfast of suet pudding and gravy.

Bookings for a small, cheaply priced show of this kind were fairly easily obtained. After opening at a cinema in Beighton near Sheffield they worked at other similar places in the areas of Sheffield and Newcastle-on-Tyne. The cast certainly enjoyed themselves but for Lily it was a headache. Apart from the task of trying to make ends meet, there were many day-to-day working difficulties that had to be faced. As Sandy says, 'Being kids we didn't realise what it meant. There were times when we had to go to the public soup kitchen to get food, though to us this wasn't a grim experience but good fun.'

The expense and responsibility of taking such a large company on tour finally proved too much for Lily and forced her to cut down on numbers. A smaller company was formed and the tour went on under the name of 'The Happy Go Luckies' presented by Lily Tagnee. Tagnee was the name of an American vaudeville star and Lily, thinking it sounded impressive,

Mr Sandy Powell, The Ideal Scotch Comedian. Circa 1912.

adopted it. The cast comprised Lily, Sandy, Netta Ross and Tim Bobbin, all experienced performers; there were no dancing boys or girls this time. Unfortunately things did not improve and the tour limped from town to town, just existing from day to day. Disaster finally overtook them when they reached Crawcrook near Newcastle-on-Tyne to work a cinema. There was hardly any money left in the kitty. Apart from the cash needed to pay for the digs, they also wanted enough to get them to Darlington, where they were booked at the Hippodrome, which was a real theatre. A good week at Crawcrook therefore was absolutely essential. The cinema was a corru-gated-iron building situated in a field. Business there had been bad because of a heat wave which turned the corrugated-iron shanty almost into an oven. 'The Happy Go Luckies' prayed fervently for rain and their prayers were soon answered. It started to rain and it went on raining; in fact the field became so waterlogged that very few people came in, and those who did could hardly hear a word spoken or sung owing to the noise of the incessant downpour on the iron roof. The company prayed for it to stop, but in vain. In desperation Lily telephoned the management of the Hippodrome to explain their predicament and begged them to telegraph an advance pay-ment, enough to cover the fares for the company to Darlington on the following Sunday. The Hippodrome management granted her request. Then on the Saturday morning the rain stopped, but only for a short while and during the afternoon it rained again, and even heavier. By the evening the cinema was completely flooded and the show had to be cancelled.

This was the last straw and Lily felt she could not stand it any longer. The responsibility of keeping the show on the road with all its attendant worries was just too much. She and Sandy would be better off working on their own. They had a good week at Darlington and made enough to pay the artists wages and digs and to get them back home. So the company broke up and went their different ways.

Lily and Sandy now back home in Rotherham and having very little money in hand, decided to combine their talents and form a double act, and so was born the act 'Lily & Sandy'.

They entered a talent competition which was held at the Palace, Atter-cliffe in the suburbs of Sheffield. In the audience was an agent called Fred Reynolds. He had a good reputation for getting work for acts in the smaller theatres and 'Lily & Sandy' was booked for a number of dates in places like Eckington, Heanor, Coalville and other small colliery towns in the North.

One night after the first house at Hetton-le-Hole in Durham the manager came backstage and said to Sandy, 'Young man, can you do something different for the second house?' 'Certainly,' said Sandy, 'I'll do some different jokes.' 'No thanks,' replied the manager, 'I don't like you as a comic and if you can't do something different to that, we'll just have the lady on her own.' So for the rest of the week Lily did a single act and Sandy was left to wonder what it was all about.

Disillusioned and downhearted, Sandy heard that his cousin Billy was going off to stay with an uncle in Liverpool and asked whether he could join him. He was now fed up with the stage and thought he might try his hand at something else.

The two boys decided that they would go into trade on their own, so, like many small-time entrepreneurs before them, they scraped up enough money to buy a dozen boxes of matches. They found a good pitch near Lime Street Station, a very busy spot with people coming and going in great numbers, particularly during rush hours. They sold their initial stock quickly and rushed off to re-invest in further stock which sold equally quickly, leaving them with a few coppers profit. This was the life, they thought, and decided to widen the scope of their operations by selling newspapers during the evening rush hour. Their pitch was next to the

An evocative photograph of Lily and Sandy working together, spotlighted against a painted backdrop.

popular Liverpool landmark, the booth of the *Punch and Judy* man who was a great and friendly character. Sandy remembers the day when he engaged a new 'bottler'. 'Bottling' was the term used by street entertainers to describe the person who took the hat round the audience of passers-by who move on when they have seen enough. A skilled bottler made the difference between a good or bad collection and on occasions, between the entertainers eating or not eating. The most sought-after bottler was a man with one arm, the theory being that he was less likely to fiddle the takings.

When the boys had sold their stock of evening papers they went to see the shows. Cousin Billy was just as keen as Sandy about the theatre and neither of them was particular as to what kind of show they saw as long as it was a live one. It was in a repertory company at the Theatre Royal in Breck Road, Liverpool, that Sandy first saw a man who later became a big star of the music hall and a very good friend – Robb Wilton. On this occasion he played a small part, an escaped convict in a thrilling melodrama, and his wife, Florence Palmer, was the leading lady.

At the Alhambra, Morecambe, Sandy saw an act on the bill which impressed him enormously; it was the act of an artist called Gus Harris. Gus, a character comedian with a powerful singing voice was billed as 'The People's Popular Chorus Idol'. He was a top-ranking star in the North country but rarely worked in the South of England. Sandy was eleven years old when he first watched Gus Harris at work, completely fascinated with every performance he saw from the wings. It was the time of the coronation of King George V. A special song had been composed to mark the occasion and it was called 'God Save Our Sailor King'. Gus, dressed in the uniform of a naval officer, sang it with great patriotic fervour especially the chorus:

> God Save our Sailor King,
> Ruler of the Free.
> Noble King of a Noble Sire,
> Mighty King of a Great Empire.
> What 'ere your Creed may be,
> Let all your voices Ring,
> Send Him Victorious,
> God Save our Sailor King.

The line 'What 'ere your Creed may be' was really belted out, particularly the word 'Creed'. Gus was Jewish with pronounced Hebraic features, and was anxious to emphasise that one could be a loyal and patriotic subject irrespective of one's religion.

A few years later, Sandy worked with him on the same bill at the Salford Hippodrome. Billed as 'The Great Versatile Hebrew Comedian' – his big numbers were now 'Gentile and Jew' and 'The Only Yiddisher Scotsman in the Irish Fusiliers' and both were real show-stoppers. For the latter number Gus was dressed in a khaki tunic and a brightly patterned kilt, and his strong-cast features enhanced the song, the chorus of which ran:

> Sergeant Solomon Isaacstein,
> He's the pet of the Fighting Line.
> Oy, Yoi, Yoi, give three hearty Cheers,
> For the only Yiddisher Scotsman
> In the Irish Fusiliers.

Sandy regrets the passing of character comedians of the type and calibre as Gus Harris. There were many like him in the great days of music hall and each was different in style. There could be three, four, or even five comics on the same bill, yet they didn't clash with each other. Sandy feels that today there is too much 'sameness' in the material presented by comedians. He also deplores the scarcity of good speciality acts such as conjurers, acrobats, jugglers and dancers; a scarcity which he feels represents a decline in public entertainment.

Now that Sandy was back, Lily decided to put the double-act on the road again. Although work wasn't difficult to get, the salaries were small and by the time they had paid fares, digs, food, agents' commissions and sundries, there was very little left at the end of the week.

They thought their big break had come when they were seen working at the Hippodrome, Chesterfield, by a top-of-the-bill-act: Scott and Whaley the black-faced entertainers who had come over from the Theatre Royal, nearby. Backstage, they asked Lily whether the act had ever worked in London. 'No,' she replied, 'but we'd love to.' Harry Scott gave them his professional card and said that he would write a letter of recommendation to his agent in London, an important man by the name of Leo Fritz. 'Go and see him,' he said, 'I'm sure he can fix you some work.' Lily thought that this could be really something, but again there was the question of money for fares to London, and at that particular moment funds were pretty low. However, she managed to borrow enough for the journey and also an overnight stay at some modestly priced digs. One of the acts on the bill gave them an address in the Waterloo Road, and off they went with high hopes of success.

Mr Fritz welcomed them saying that he had heard from Harry Scott; it was nice to know that he had kept his promise. The agent asked Lily how they worked and she told him that Sandy worked in the style of Harry Weldon and that their double-act was something like 'Jack and Evelyn' who were a famous act that specialised in burlesque comedy. Mr Fritz said that it was just the sort of thing he was looking for, and that he was able to give them an immediate booking – a trial week at the Hippodrome, Rotherham. Lily thought it best not to mention that she had to borrow money to make the journey from Rotherham to London just to get a week's work in their own home town. They worked the date, but it is sad to record that the act was not a success.

In August 1914 war was declared. Theatres and cinemas stayed open and work was plentiful. On the bill at a cinema in West Houghton were two acts, Lily and Sandy and a talented young lady named Gracie Stansfield. Little did they realise that nearly thirty years later Sandy would be making gramophone records with this girl, when they were both stars; he as Sandy Powell and she as Gracie Fields. Sandy remembers that particular week because it was Gracie who first persuaded him to wear spectacles. They were waiting at a stop for a bus to take them to the theatre. One approached and Gracie asked, 'Isn't that our bus, Sandy?' He replied, 'I'm not sure, I can't see the number.' 'You can't? Then you ought to wear glasses.' So next morning, they went to the opticians where Sandy was fitted with a pair; and from then on, thanks to Gracie, he regularly wore glasses off stage.

A couple of London dates at last materialised. The very first week they worked in town was at the Palace, Bow, a small theatre in the East End, and the second at the famous Bedford in Camden Town; both dates were booked by the well-known agent Harry Day. He told Lily that he was sending out a touring company of the successful London Hippodrome revue *Business as Usual*. The stars of the London production were Harry Tate, Violet Lorraine and Shirley Kellogg. On tour the Harry Tate part was to be played by Harry Piddock, and Mr Day wanted Sandy to play the part of one of Harry Tate's 'Pa-Pa' boys, a precocious brat dressed in a short Eton jacket (then popularly referred to as 'bum-freezers') to be supplied by Mr Day. Lily had a crucial decision to make: the double-act was working quite steadily but, on the other hand, it would be an opportunity for Sandy to work with top-class artists. Lily, as ever a good and unselfish parent, signed the contract on his behalf.

Business as Usual opened at the Devonshire Park Theatre in Eastbourne. During the first performance in a sketch called 'Fortifying the Garden' (in preparation to defend our shores against invasion by the Huns), Sandy was on stage awaiting the entrance of the principal comedian, who had missed his cue. Then into his mind flashed the thought that this was his opportunity to step in and save the show. He plunged into a string of jokes about his mother-in-law and domestic comedy patter that were quite unsuitable coming from a boy of his age. A deathly silence followed his feeble quips and the leading lady, Ouida McDermott, marched on stage and promptly boxed his ears. By this time Harry Piddock had made his belated entrance and although he picked up the threads expertly, the sketch was killed and tottered on to a sad climax. Sandy who had thought that his prompt action had saved the day was further humiliated when the touring manager, Charles Henry, asked him 'what the devil was he playing at?' 'You ruined that scene' he yelled and gave Sandy notice on the spot. It was a shattering experience to be given the sack on the very first night. The following week the company moved on to the Pleasure Gardens Theatre, Folkestone, where Sandy worked out his notice. After the last show on Saturday night, Sandy and his mother walked back to their cheap lodgings through the blacked-out streets, desperately unhappy and at times in tears. It was such a disastrous end to what was going to be Sandy's opportunity to get into 'the big time'.

When they arrived back in Rotherham they were broke and extremely apprehensive of the future. Lily went back to working her single act and Sandy went to stay with an uncle in Manchester. He had to get a job and after looking around found one in the Metropolitan-Vickers factory, where he only lasted a week. His next job was at British Westinghouse at Trafford Park, but his stay there was equally brief and he concluded that factory work was not for him. Sandy was to discover that he had many uncles and that one of them had a greengrocer's shop. His cousin Billy and he once again decided that they would go into trade. They managed to secure a handcart and with the help of the indulgent greengrocer-uncle filled it up with fruit and vegetables and trundled it around the streets. It was a risky enterprise and after a couple of weeks the novelty wore off. Billy remembered that there was yet another uncle who lived in Blackpool; the idea of working at a seaside resort during the summer months was an alluring prospect, so off they went to Blackpool.

Sandy found a job escorting a string of donkeys safely back and forth from their stables and the beach. Cousin Billy found employment at the Pleasure Beach Amusement Park as an attendant at a mechanical ride called 'Witching Waves'.

The Palace at Blackpool was a great attraction for the boys and they went as often as possible to see the great entertainers of the day. When Harry Weldon played there it was a cause for great excitement and they played truant from their jobs, so eager were they to see their music-hall idol. Their absence from work resulted eventually in their getting the sack. Undaunted, however, they made their way back to Liverpool to stay with an uncle who was much relieved to hear that the boys were there to look for work. They found their way to the docks where they became excited by thoughts of sailing to foreign lands. Hearing that there were vacancies on the S.S. *St Louis* bound for New York, they applied for work on the ship. Billy was signed on but Sandy was rejected because he was too young. When Billy heard this he said he wasn't going without his cousin. It turned out to be a lucky break because, *en route* to America, the S.S. *St Louis* was sunk by enemy action.

The lads returned home again, and Lily and Sandy went out to work a tour of cinemas and theatres in the north of England and Scotland. They worked in the Liverpool area, and at the Westminster Theatre had the rare experience of working for the first time on a stage with gas footlights. At the Empire, Greenock in Scotland, Sandy had his first experience of 'getting the bird'. This theatre had a reputation in the profession as a very tough theatre to work. The gallery came right out to within a few feet of the proscenium. A close-mesh wire netting was stretched between them to prevent things being thrown into the orchestra pit and stage below. The audience had their own particular favourites, especially the Scottish acts, and were usually very hostile to 'foreigners' like the English. Scottish stars, with very few exceptions, never worked south of the border and very few English acts ventured north of it. They simply wouldn't listen to Sandy

From top left, clockwise: Scott and Whaley, Sir Oswald Stoll, George Formby Snr, Wish Wynne, Bransby Williams, Arthur Roberts, Harry Weldon. Centre: Hetty King.

and every time he made an entrance there were shouts of 'Get off!' In the
end Lily had to do her single act.

The disappointment at his rough treatment at Greenock was soon forgotten when Sandy got his first break into pantomime at the age of fifteen
and discovered the joy of working to children. It was a field in which he was
later to become a great star.

Although pantomimes provided many weeks work, the rest of the year
had to be taken into account. More variety work came in for the better-class
dates and while at the City Varieties, Leeds (later to become the home of
the BBC's famous television show *Those Were the Days*) Lily and Sandy
were asked to go across to the Empire Dewsbury to deputize for Wee
Georgie Wood who was topping the bill there. They made a hit and one
night a note came backstage from Bertram Montague, a London agent,
asking them to meet him the next morning at the Queens Hotel. It was
actually pure chance that had brought Montague to the Empire that night,
but it turned out to be a really big break for Sandy and a turning point in
his career.

When they met Montague they were surprised to find that he was quite
a young man, not many years older than Sandy in fact, but he was an agent
from London and that was important. It was obvious that Bert Montague
had recognised the talent and potential of young Sandy. He told him that if
he came on to his books and allowed Montague to represent him, he could
get him an immediate two weeks' trial on Stoll theatres and was confident
that he could get him the rest of the tour. Lily was again faced with the
prospect of splitting up their double act and letting Sandy go out with his
single. She decided to let him have another try because the Stoll tour gave
him a chance of breaking into the big-time of music hall.

The first Stoll date was in London at the Shepherd's Bush Empire (now
a BBC television theatre), the salary was fifteen pounds a week which was
pretty good for those days. Oswald Stoll, who in 1919 became Sir Oswald
Stoll, always attended the first house at 'The Bush' on Saturdays, and after
the show he sent a note to say how pleased he was with Sandy's act, and
that he would give him the rest of the Stoll tour. This was marvellous
news, confirming Bert Montague's confidence and it led to what was to
become a very happy association between them. The second Stoll date
was at the Empire, Ardwick Green, Manchester. The salary for this date
and other provincial Stoll theatres was seventeen pounds ten shillings
a week. In London there were the 'Empires' at Hackney, Chiswick and
Shepherds Bush. In other parts of the country the Stoll theatres were
named Empire, Hippodrome or Palace, Sandy played them all and became
firmly established as a standard act. Stoll had said that Sandy would one
day become a star and he was proved right. The young up-and-coming
Sandy was pushed by Stoll and given good billing whenever possible. At
Chiswick Empire he was second top to the great international star, the
French clown Grock, and at the Bristol Hippodrome he was also billed
second top to another big star of the day, the fine character sketch actress

and impressionist Wish Wynne. It was now quite evident that Sandy was going places. Oswald Stoll himself was very helpful to young performers and gave them every chance, and particularly to Sandy because his material was clean. If there was one thing that Stoll detested it was blue material. There were many who thought that Stoll was too strict and insistent in demanding a higher standard of refinement, and that he was watering down the rich blood of music hall. This was an argument that Stoll resisted vigorously and made it clear that he had built beautiful theatres and wanted them to be places where a man could take his family without embarrassment. This was a view which Sandy heartily supported and does so to this day.

The dressing-room notices in Stoll theatres were much discussed in the profession, and one such notice that caused controversy said 'Please do not ask for complimentary tickets. If your friends won't pay to come in to see you, you are not good enough to work in this theatre.' This notice really put the cat among the pigeons because artists thought that working in the theatre gave them a right to free tickets for their friends. (It was common practice for the artists to use their professional visiting cards to gain free admission to shows in other theatres and even to cinemas.)

Being a teenage star during the First World War brought its problems. The nation was engulfed by a wave of patriotism and everywhere young men were answering the call to fight for King and Country. Sandy's comedy makeup was heavy, disguising his youthful looks, and very often audiences would call out during Sandy's act 'Why aren't you in the army?' It was thought that anyone old enough to be on the stage was old enough to be in the Forces. Stoll, who was anxious not to offend his patrons had an enlargement made of Sandy's birth certificate for display in the foyer of the theatre.

All the artists performed in charity shows, military camps and hospitals and endeavoured to help the war effort as much as possible.

Dates on the other tours were also coming in nicely and sometimes there were two theatres to work each night. This was called 'doubling' and although it was pretty strenuous work, it meant extra money.

Sandy is probably the only artist still working today who actually performed on the same bill as such great stars as Arthur Roberts, Little Tich, Fay Robina, Marie Lloyd, George Mozart, Bransby Williams, George Formby Snr, Whit Cunliffe, Tom Costello, Charles Whittle, Wilkie Bard, Robb Wilton, Vesta Tilley and Hetty King. He still thinks that Hetty King was the finest artist he ever worked with.

Sandy was now working regularly, and with more money coming in, made sure Lily was well provided for. He also felt that it was about time that he owned a motor car; apart from anything else, it would be a fine status symbol. His first car was bought from a motoring establishment in Shaftesbury Avenue. It was a large, flashy-looking Bedford-Buick that was reputed to have belonged to the American vaudeville star, Fred Duprez – just right for a young up-and-coming star who wanted to create an impression. The car salesman taught him to drive, just one lesson given in Tottenham Court Road, in the heart of London's West End. There were no driving tests and if you bought a car you could drive right away with nothing to stop you, except possibly a lamp post, if your driving was a little speculative. Sandy however did not do too badly, and, although a novice driver, decided to take a chance, and on the following Sunday morning set off for Leicester, where he was booked to appear for the week at the Palace Theatre, an important Stoll date.

When he got to Edgeware, just outside London, he came to a steep incline called Brockley Hill. The car was about half-way up the hill when it came to a shuddering halt. It could have been Sandy's inexperienced driving or a mechanical fault. The fact was he was stuck on the hill, and not knowing what to do, he had to suffer the indignity of begging a tow from a passing motorist. He coasted down the other side of the hill and soon the motor was again running sweetly; from there on progress was steady but sure. He arrived at the outskirts of Leicester and was preparing for a grand arrival at the theatre, when a tyre burst. He finished up by trundling the punctured tyre, like a kid bowling a hoop, to the nearest garage. It was a sad letdown.

Sandy was just eighteen when he had the great thrill of topping the bill at a major theatre – the Palace in Blackpool. This was a rare distinction in those days for one so young. Another big break came when he worked the Pavilion in Glasgow (this time playing a Scottish date with great success) and word came across from the Empire, which was Glasgow's largest and most important theatre, that their top of the bill, Harry Weldon, had been taken ill and they wanted Sandy to deputize for him. This was the ultimate, and the fulfilment of his childhood dreams.

However, it turned out even better, for he was asked to take over the star spot, as well as the star's time of twenty-five minutes. This really gave him the chance to show himself to the best advantage, and brought him all the Moss Empire dates.

However, on 30th April 1918, he received his 'call-up papers' from the War Office. Another young man working on the same bill at the Palace, Southampton, got his papers at the same time. He was the straight man in an act called 'The Juggling Beaucaires'. Many years later he was to gain fame as 'Monsewer Eddie Gray', the comedy juggler and marvellous buffoon with the 'Crazy Gang'.

Neither was happy about being called up. Eddie had a brainwave and asked Sandy if he smoked. 'Not much', was the reply, 'hardly at all, in fact.' Eddie said that he remembered someone telling him that if you smoked a lot just before going into a 'medical', your heart would bang so much that you would be turned down. They did this, nearly choking themselves in the process. Sandy needn't have bothered for he was rejected anyway, and graded C3!

Towards the end of 1918, the losses in the armed forces were so great that they started to call up all and sundry. Sandy received notice to report to the Army Depot in his home town, Rotherham, on 11th of November. At 11 a.m. on that day, the Armistice was declared and Sandy didn't have to go. They had won the war without him!

Fifty Years in Panto

Three things are needed at Christmastime,
Plum pudding, Beef and Pantomime;
Folk can resist the other two,
Without the latter, none can do.

THIS old saying describes Sandy's approach to what he considered the ideal Christmas and New Year entertainment for children, the traditional, perennial English pantomime. The simple plot loosely based on a universally loved fairy tale, a story in which the children could feel themselves completely involved in what was happening on the stage. In this situation the children want to hiss the villain, cheer the principal boy, usually played by a lady whose dignity and gallantry is a gem of theatrical flamboyance, to love the heroine, the acme of charm and tenderness, and of course to laugh uproariously at the irascible dame, a man in 'skirts'. There were the thrills of the speciality acts, dragged in for no reason, and the excitement of the magical transformations, colourful scenery, and beautiful costumes and dresses. Pantomime possessed the power to turn the most blasé and cynical member of an audience into a cheerful, whistling and singing youngster again. In short it was a big party.

Pantomime fitted Sandy's outlook and personality, he exuded warmth and friendliness, and as a children's comedian, was a natural. A few minutes after taking the stage he introduced a gag which became a conspicuous part of the performance. Just to reassure himself that the children were still there, he would from time to time say 'Hello children' and back would come an answering roar from the audience, including the elderly ladies and gentlemen, 'Hello Sandy'. The interpretation of the various characters he played made it easy for the Children to identify themselves with him.

Sandy's favourite role was that of Buttons, the page-boy in *Cinderella*. It is generally considered the classic pantomime role and it combines humour and pathos in the best tradition. The children understood and sympathised with his hopeless love for the entrancing Cinders and laughed at his homely fun.

He was fifteen when Teddy Jazon of the Liverpool-based agents Jazon & Montgomery saw the 'Lily and Sandy' act and gave them the booking for *Cinderella* at the Rotunda in Liverpool. Sandy was to play one of the Broker's men and a special part was written for Lily so that the double-act could be used in one of the scenes. It was working with the very experienced cast of this show including Leo Fields and Fred Martinett that gave Sandy the insight into pantomime that was to stand him in such good stead in later years. He also discovered that in the smaller touring shows that it was customary for the lesser artists to do small parts in addition to their own. His first taste of this was when he was given the job of 'back-legs' of the elephant. After the first shock of being enclosed in a smelly skin with another man who had also been 'press-ganged' into playing 'front-legs', he found that it was good fun. The principal boy (Prince Charming) was played by Joan Tate, the Sisters Katrina were the Ugly Sisters and Lillian Erroll was Cinderella. The show toured for some weeks, and the agents were so pleased with Lily and Sandy they rebooked them for the following year, again in *Cinderella*, with Sandy repeating his role as broker's man, but achieving promotion in the elephant rôle, by being selected to play 'front-legs' with the responsibility for manipulating the elephant's trunk, which in reality was a cloth-covered broom handle!

At this time Sandy was just sixteen and desperately anxious to extend the range of his work. He tried hard to get into as many small parts and other pieces in the show. The scene that closed the first half started with a straight

Sandy's first pantomine in 1915. He is standing on the far right with his hand on Lily's shoulder.

ballet performed by the dancing girls. It was really an excuse for the comics to turn it into a 'cod ballet', – a burlesque designed to get big laughs and send the patrons out feeling happy for their drinks at the theatre bars during the interval. Buttons was played by an excellent comedian called George Hyams. He was the first principal and played a major part in getting laughs from the quite ludicrous cod ballet. There was one thing that George Hyams resented, and that was somebody else getting the laughs while he was on stage. At rehearsals Sandy thought that he would like to get in on the burlesque ballet, so he asked Mr Jazon if he could join in. It was on the first night at the Kings, Longsight, near Manchester, and Sandy joined the scene much to the annoyance of George Hyams, especially as he improvised some antics of his own and the audience responded heartily. When the curtain came down at the end of the show, Hyams buttonholed Sandy and took him over to Mr Jazon, who was standing in the wings. 'Mr Jazon,' said Hyams, 'before we go any further I want to know one thing. Who is the principal comic in this show? Teddy Jazon snapped back 'The one that gets the most bloody laughs!'

Sandy did well enough to earn another engagement with the Jazon & Montgomery pantomime for the following 1917–18 season. This pantomime was *Sinbad the Sailor* and he was given the part of Tinbad, a simple lovable lad, a rôle that demanded some pathos as well as comedy. It was the type of character that Sandy developed in the ensuing years in a style that was unmistakably his own. The show opened at the Pavilion, Liverpool, then went on tour for a few weeks. The experience gained working with Jazon & Montgomery for three seasons was of inestimable value. It led him to a new experience – working in a Scottish pantomime just after the First World War, during the 1918–19 season.

Pantomimes usually opened on Boxing Day and carried over into the New Year, playing as many weeks at a theatre as business would justify. A season in pantomime could mean three to six weeks or it could mean a run of two to three months. The original show could be followed by either a short or long tour of other theatres, sometimes depending upon the availability of the stars. Scottish pantomimes ran longer than any others in the British Isles, and Sandy's first was in Richard Waldon's *Handy Andy* at the Royal Princess's Theatre in Glasgow. At that time The Princess was considered to be the home of Scottish pantomime, which was far removed from the traditional English pantomime; it was more like a revue. The action, scenery and costumes were not 'period' and while one sketch was a burlesque of a police-court scene, another took place in a telephone exchange. Sandy played the central character, a sort of Simple Simon, but in one of his spots he donned a pirate costume and sang Billy Merson's immortal song 'Yacki Hickie Dula'. He also worked a spot with two popular Scottish comedians 'McGregor and Hood' and many laughs came from Sandy's inability to comprehend their strong Glaswegian dialect.

Sandy's next excursion into pantomime was with one of the great names in music hall, John Tiller. It was John Tiller who originated the idea of training a troupe of girls to dance with the precision of guardsmen. 'Tiller Girls' were and still are internationally famous. Many other dancing troupes based their style, routine and training on the Tiller troupe. John Tiller's *Red Riding Hood* at the Theatre Royal, Hanley, was a kind of Robin Hood story with Sandy playing the Baron's page-boy.

John Tiller re-engaged Sandy for the following, 1921–2 season with another similar part to play, that of Simple Simon in *Jack and Jill* at the Empire, Sheffield. This was the show that John Tiller had produced the previous year at the Empire, Newcastle-on-Tyne, when the great comedian George Formby (father of George Formby, the ukelele-playing comedian of later years) had played the 'Simple Simon' part.

This was an important show for Sandy because it was the first time that he had worked with really top-flight artists in pantomime. Tom D. Newall, one of pantomime's great stars, played Dame and in this show Sandy also had the experience of working with a male principal boy who was a big star of the day; Fred Barnes was very good-looking, dressed immaculately, had an easy manner and a very fine singing voice. Gaining confidence, Sandy found that he was capable of holding his own in the best of company, it also became obvious that he was a natural for pantomime, so it was not surprising that he claimed the attention of top producers. Francis Laidler, deservedly known as 'King of Pantomime', booked him for the role of Peter the Page in his lavish production of *Cinderella* at the Theatre Royal, Leeds, a show of major importance. Sandy signed the contract in August, and thought that, as was the custom, his next contact would be at rehearsals a couple of weeks prior to opening. But he was surprised when Mr Laidler asked for a meeting in October, at which he was asked to submit the gags that he wanted to use in the show. These were fully discussed and agreed upon, so that when rehearsals came round no time was wasted because each comic knew exactly what could be used.

Laidler was a traditionalist, and in his pantomimes a character was not allowed to 'step out of the picture'. It was against all tradition for an artist to address the audience directly, or to encourage a response from them. Sandy explained to Mr Laidler that he had a sketch in which the umbrella he was carrying was placed against the proscenium arch, and he would ask the children to keep an eye on it, and to warn him if anyone tried to steal it while he was busy elsewhere. He assured Mr Laidler that it was a great gag, a gag that was repeated many times, and got yells each time. Mr Laidler replied that he had never allowed anyone to do that kind of thing in his pantomimes. Sandy pleaded with him for permission to try it and if it didn't register with the children, he would cut it out right away. Mr Laidler reluctantly agreed to this, and luckily for Sandy it turned out to be one of the funniest situations in the show.

Sandy was the first comedian to work in this way with the children in the audience; it later became standard practice, and many other comedians started using it in their own acts.

Gwladys Stanley, the principal boy, headed a strong cast, with Sandy

Tom D. Newall wishes Sandy the very best. The Empire, Sheffield, 1921.

as second principal. Aimy Verity was a charming Cinders, the popular north country comedians Jimmy Pullin and Fred Anderson were hilarious as the Ugly Sisters and Leslie Barker was Dandini. Press reports were very favourable, and stated that 'Mr Powell's conception of Peter the Page was bound to open up great possibilities for this rising young comedian and that he was sure to succeed.'

One night, the stagedoor-keeper brought Sandy a message that a Mr Cochran would like a few words with him after the show. It was the great impresario, Charles B. Cochran, who after formal introductions told Sandy that he liked his work and that there was a great future ahead for him, but asked if he could take advice. Cochran told him that he thought Sandy should give up using heavy comedy makeup, dispense with thick eyebrows, red noses, baggy trousers and 'those funny boots'. Cochran also said that one of these days he would like to see him and be able to say 'Sandy Powell you have become a star.' Many years later, in 1938, when working in pantomime at the Palace, Manchester, Charles B. Cochran went backstage and visited Sandy again, and reminded him of their meeting fifteen years before, and that he had obviously taken his advice. He was satisfied that his judgement had been right, for after watching Sandy that night he could now say, 'Sandy Powell you are a star.'

The show played to capacity audiences during a record-breaking run for the theatre, from Christmas right through to the following Easter, 1923. A highly satisfied Laidler immediately booked Sandy to appear the following season at his Princes Theatre in Bradford.

It used to be customary in pantomime that during the week before closing, the principals were each allowed a 'Benefit Night', which gave the patrons a chance to show their appreciation of the artists efforts to please them. The success or otherwise of a Benefit Night was the measure of an artist's popularity. They were occasions when the management presented gifts to the performers and staff. The artists also gave presents to each other. Benefit nights usually packed houses and the box-office receipts, less a generous percentage for the management to cover their overheads, produced a handsome sum for the beneficiaries. In a special handbill printed for the occasion Miss Gwladys Stanley was described as the 'Queen of English Pantomime' and the Monday performance was allocated for her Benefit Night, while the Thursday performance was given to Sandy. The printed handbills stated that on the Benefit Nights the bill would include 'Enormous Added Attractions'. It transpired that many stars were booked to appear on Miss Stanley's night, but none for Sandy's. He, therefore, asked his mother to appear as his 'Surprise Guest Artist', and a cloth was fixed up with the words of the songs and choruses she used to sing in her act. When Sandy introduced her as 'Lily Le Main – my mother', it tore the place apart and the packed audience joined in the choruses with great enthusiasm. The night ended with a demonstration by students from Leeds University, who had booked over a hundred seats for the performance. At the end of the evening they stood outside the stage door chanting, 'We want

Sandy,' and when he came out, still in his stage clothes, they hoisted him on to their shoulders and carried him along the main street singing 'For He's a Jolly Good Fellow' and finally delivered him back to the theatre. Miss Stanley was not amused and thought that the whole affair had been pre-arranged. It was in fact a great surprise to Sandy. He was very popular with the students and a regular attender at their functions, particularly at their amateur-boxing shows and other sporting events. As a result of this incident ill-feeling developed to a point that on the last night pantomime tradition was broken in a most unpleasant way. Panto 'last nights' were usually fun nights when the roles were changed around, the principal boy playing the part of the broker's man and one of the comedians playing the principal girl's role. There was plenty of gagging and the audience enjoyed it as much as the performers. In most pantomimes it was usually played 'off the cuff', but in the Laidler productions it was different; the show was properly rehearsed, for Laidler never allowed anything impromptu or un-rehearsed to appear on his stage. He had a regular 'call' when the exchange roles were run through, but on this particular occasion Sandy was left out. Laidler told him curtly that he was not needed at the rehearsal and he was not to join in the gags, but to play strictly to the script. This was a great blow to Sandy, who told Laidler that he would never work for him again, and would ask his agent to get the next season's engagement with Laidler cancelled. The startled Mr Laidler replied, 'Young man, the next time you play Moss Empires you will remember me.' It may have been a coincidence, but a few weeks later Sandy worked a Moss date at the Victoria Palace in London, and he was put on first turn and his act was timed for three minutes. This was the first and only time that Sandy had a serious argument with the management.

By nature he was not quarrelsome but this episode had hurt him deeply. When some time later the music publisher Bert Feldman 'phoned Sandy to go in and see him, he had a suspicion as to what it was about. Feldman told him that he was sorry Sandy had fallen out with Francis Laidler and advised him to be a little more understanding.

It was many years later when Sandy happened to be walking down Charing Cross Road in London that he saw Francis Laidler walking to-wards him and each instinctively looked each other straight in the eye, put out his hand and shook firmly. Laidler suggested that they should celebrate and what about Sandy bringing his *Road Show* to the Alhambra, Bradford? Sandy was taken aback; he thought that Laidler's suggestion to 'celebrate' meant a drink and a friendly chat, instead Laidler had turned the occasion into an opportunity for him to get the big attraction that Sandy undoubtedly was into his theatres.

The seal of Sandy's pantomime fame was stamped when he was booked to play Buttons in Cinderella for the 1924–5 season by the man who was known affectionately by the stars as 'The Guvnor', the owner of the Alexandra Theatre in Birmingham, Leon Salberg.

The 'Alec' provided a marvellous shop window for Sandy. This production by David Cochrane not only helped Sandy, but also helped to establish The Alec as an important centre for pantomime. In the old days The Alec pantomime was noted for 'good rough fun', but a new epoch began when Sandy went in for the first time there and started a trend of humour which, while losing nothing in effective robustness, was free from any offensiveness. The Alexandra, together with Philip Rodway's Theatre Royal, made Birmingham, from the point of view of the artists, the Mecca of pantomime.

The cast included Nellie Wigley, a very distinguished Prince Charming, Rona Ray an entrancing Cinders, Sonia Seale a lively Dandini, the Brothers Obo as superb Ugly Sisters, and an uproarious Harlequinade by the Cyril Boganny Troupe, and of course Sandy Powell who, according to the influential *Birmingham Gazette*, was voted 'The Children's Comedian of the Year'.

Leon Salberg was born in Poland and was a quiet and modest man. He spoke English with a thick foreign accent, described by Sandy as 'a sort of fractured English'. When Salberg bought the Alexandra, he knew little about theatre, but was wise enough to employ experts to do the things he didn't understand. He built The Alec from being at best a somewhat mediocre theatre into a first-class house, capable of staging top-class pantomime and reputable drama. When Salberg died in 1937, his son Derek, in true tradition, took over the business and carried it on in the way his father would have wished.

Salberg's Saturday Night Parties became famous as an after-show rendezvous for the stars and their friends. Another Salberg innovation was his popular annual 'Alexandra Pantomime Banquet and Dance' to which the whole company and staff were invited, together with the Guvnor's personal guests, business friends and artists from all the shows working in Birmingham at the time.

Sandy remembers the occasion. He was invited to attend a meeting of the principal comics in the Guvnor's office. Comics in company with other comics are usually very wary of each other, always wondering what the other fellow might do. They made sure that they were fast with a gag and even faster with the quick return that must top the other man's jokes. A meeting such as this could quickly develop into a cut-and-thrust contest which on the surface might seem friendly, but where the 'daggers were drawn', ready for speedy use if necessary. Leon had wisely discovered that a comics' meeting, before rehearsals, if handled with tact and good sense, could make all the difference between a happy run or one marred by illfeeling and bickering. His method was quite simple, the meeting never started before the champagne was produced, and during the preliminaries glasses were filled and refilled, and in no time everyone was feeling relaxed and falling over each other to be cooperative. The Dame, broker's men, King and all the speciality comedy artists became mellow and friendly and did not try to grab the best gags for themselves. It was not until the next

RICHMOND THEATRE

THE THEATRE ON THE GREEN

Direction: F. J. BUTTERWORTH   PHONE 0088   General Manager : A. J. MATTHEWS

2-30   TWICE DAILY   6-15

5-10 p.m.   APPROXIMATE FINISHING TIME   8-55 p.m.

COMMENCING SATURDAY, 23RD DECEMBER

GRAND CHRISTMAS PANTOMIME

CINDERELLA

WITH A STAR CAST, INCLUDING THE FAMOUS COMEDIAN,
"CAN YOU HEAR ME MOTHER"

SANDY POWELL

AS "BUTTONS"

"PRINCE CHARMING"
BABS DUDLEY

"DANDINI"
KATIE HUGHES

"VINOLIA"
ETHYL DAIMLER

SPECIALITIES BY
DEMAIN

THE SPALLAS

MARIETTA GIRLS

"THE BARON"
HARRY EMERIC

"CINDERELLA"
JOAN RANDAL

"LUSCIOUS"
AUDREY KNIGHT

SPECIALITIES BY
DUKE AND **DE SAXE**

SHELLEY AND **CLARE**

MORGAN JUVENILES

SEE THE FOREST GLADE — THE FAIRY DELL THE BALL ROOM — THE PRINCE'S PALACE

CINDERELLA'S CRYSTAL COACH DRAWN BY DRAKE'S CREAM PONIES

BOX OFFICE 10 a.m. to 8 p.m.

PRICES (Including Tax) :—

ORCHESTRA STALLS 6/-   CENTRE STALLS 4/-   BACK STALLS 2/-   BALCONY 1/-

BOXES £1 10 0   DRESS CIRCLE 6/-   BACK CIRCLE 4/-   BOXES £1 5 0

HOLDING 5   HOLDING 4

Sandy as 'Buttons' in Cinderella *at the Richmond Theatre.*

morning that the crowd of tough pros realised they had been kidded into sacrificing their own selfish fancies for the betterment of the show. Nevertheless, they admired the Guvnor all the more for his shrewdness.

The *Souvenir Book of Words* was sold to patrons for the princely sum of sixpence. It was a sixty-page booklet with a synopsis of the scenes, cast of characters, every word spoken in the pantomime, and photographs of the management and the entire cast including the dancing girls. It was therefore no surprise that producers insisted on performers sticking strictly to the script. The theatre-goers could well be offended by a character inserting his own lines and thus breaking the rhythm in their reading of the book. It could be compared with the position of music enthusiasts who wished to follow the score or libretto at a symphony concert or opera performance. Philip Rodway of the Theatre Royal in Birmingham was a stickler for strict adherence to the book and would not allow the slightest variation. It was a difficult rule for some artists to follow, and especially so during a long run, when they would want to ad-lib to avoid getting bored with their part.

Although Salberg respected tradition he was prepared to bend the rules to help business at the box office. An astute entrepreneur, he promoted the idea of filling his theatre with groups of people from the large industrial firms in and around Birmingham. Sandy used to get notes from the front office asking him to alter his script to get in a mention of the name of a well-known personality, or large party in the audience. It gave the show a personal touch, a lot of laughs, and was very good for business.

Sandy's professional career was given a big boost when, the following season, he worked for Salberg again, playing Buttons at the Kings Theatre, Hammersmith. There he made some important contacts and received encouragement from the redoubtable Julian Wylie. Wylie was a great producer and a veritable giant among the 'Kings of Pantomime'. The list of his productions is almost without equal in the theatre. He was for a time an important agent and considered to be a supreme judge of talent; a man of ideas and probably the first agent to institute a special 'Ideas Department' within his office. He advised and groomed artists and had the reputation of being a star-maker. Sandy was therefore thrilled when a message came backstage that Mr Julian Wylie was out front and would like to see him after the show. Later in Sandy's dressing-room Mr Wylie told him that he was going to pay him one of the greatest compliments he had ever paid to a comedian. He told Sandy that he was the second-best Buttons he had ever seen, then asked him if he knew who he considered the best. Sandy assumed rightly that he was referring to Harry Weldon.

Julian Wylie was a director of the powerful Wylie & Tate Agency, as was Bert Feldman. It was Feldman who persuaded Wylie to go to the Kings that night; and he sent also another director, the powerful and influential Ernest Edelsten, there later to watch Sandy at work. Edelsten had an abrasive manner; he also had an unerring eye for potential stars. He was tough but honest, and handled his artists very skilfully. Sandy was told that Edelsten wanted to see him and to make sure he was right on time for the appointment. Edelsten wasted no time on preliminaries and came straight to the point. He said: 'Mr Powell I can make you a big star, but there are certain things that I insist you do for me. Will you do them?' Sandy replied politely, 'Tell me what they are Mr Edelsten and I will do them if I can.' Edelsten told him that to begin with there was the question of the comic who worked with Sandy. 'You will have to get rid of him,' he said. 'You allow him to get too many laughs.' He made it clear to Sandy that when he was on stage he must not provide other comics with the opportunities to get laughs. 'You must be quite ruthless,' he told Sandy. The comic in question was Al Maurice. It would be very simple, Edelston said, all that Sandy had to do was to tell Mr Wylie he couldn't work with Maurice and leave the rest to him. Edelsten made it clear that if Sandy didn't go along with his suggestion, the conversation could be disregarded and the whole matter forgotten. Sandy thanked Mr Edelsten for his offer, but as far as Al Maurice was concerned he simply couldn't do that to him, and that the matter would have to be forgotten. It was to Edelsten's credit he never held Sandy's rebuff against him and in fact shortly afterwards Wylie & Tate booked Sandy for many of their big shows, with the blessing of Mr Edelsten.

After another pantomime season with Salberg at the Wimbledon Theatre in London, Sandy returned to Birmingham for the 1928–9 season at the Alexandra, where he was the top of the bill. It was the tradition that the principal boy, usually a famous female star, was the big name on the bill, but this time it was Sandy's Idle Jack that was featured in *Dick Whittington*. The show was elaborately mounted and brilliantly staged by F. V. Maxwell-Stewart. The Birmingham papers the *Post* and the *Gazette* reported that Sandy had confirmed the high hopes raised by his previous appearance at the Alec, and that his Idle Jack was even better than his earlier success as Buttons in *Cinderella*, which was praise indeed. Kitty Franklin was a smart and dashing hero, Billy Matchett outstanding as Susan the dame, Harry Gilmore proved that he was one of the best 'Cats' in the profession. Rolando Martin, Frank Victor and the brilliant simultaneous dancers Rich and Galvin completed a first-rate cast.

Rolando Martin was a man who impressed Sandy very much. He did one gag in which his arms grew longer and longer as he held them up outstretched. He saw that Sandy was fascinated and said, 'This could be good for you Sandy, would you like me to show you how it is made and how to work it?' So for the next few mornings they met in Rolando's dressing-room and together they made the apparatus for Sandy who asked, 'Can I use this at some future date, and will you please accept this?' He offered Rolando ten pounds, but the old gentleman refused it saying, 'I don't want anything for it, it is not my gag, I saw it when working in a circus when I was quite young. I won't be using it much longer, you are a young man, Sandy, I would like you to have it.' Sandy however, insisted until Rolando finally accepted the money. He did not use the apparatus until he saw the film in which Al Jolson sang 'Sonny Boy', and he immediately thought of the long-arms gag. He had a black hood made, in which holes for the eyes and mouth were neatly cut out, and then rehearsing hard on a routine, he finished up with a comedy gem that proved a real winner, one that he would never have had if he had not seen and worked with dear Rolando, and to whom he was ever grateful.

Sandy's photograph was now prominently displayed in the *Souvenir Book of Words*, which still comprised sixty pages and cost sixpence. There was proof that theatre parties had greatly increased in popularity and the evidence of this was seen in a copy of a programme, still in Sandy's possession, which contains 'suggestion notes' from the management on almost every other page, for the audience to join in the show. Such an example was: 'Please gag about Captain Darby, Chairman of the British Legion Branch at the Austin Works, whenever the artist taking the part of the Captain in the show appears.'

In 1933, after nine consecutive seasons with Salberg, Sandy decided to launch out on his own in pantomime and bought the entire production of *Cinderella* from Salberg, including scenery, costumes and 'book'. He tailored it for a music-hall tour, building the show around himself. He was now a big name in pantomime and he banked on his personal appeal and

The only dame ever featured in a wheelchair! The Lyceum, Newport, 1958.

popularity to bring in the customers rather than relying on big-star names to support him. Star performers were very often temperamental and invariably demanded large salaries, they could create problems and Sandy felt that he would be better off with a cast of seasoned performers. He chose the cast carefully with Betty Errol as Cinders, Gaby Joyce as her Prince Charming, Peggy Novak as Dandini, The Brothers Obo as the Ugly Sisters, Frank Lorden as Baron Brokenup, Alec Ross and the Graham Brothers as the broker's men, the sixteen De Vere Babes, and specialities such as Dawson's Canary Choir, Gyer's Crystal Fountains and Drake's Four Cream Ponies. The Stoll management were happy to book the show to open on Boxing Day 1933 for two weeks at the Shepherds Bush Empire and to follow with further two weeks at the Hackney Empire. Sandy arranged that after an intensive rehearsal in London, the company would do a week at the Hippodrome, Southend, in order to get the show running smoothly before the London opening. It was unusual to open a week before Boxing Day, which was always the traditional opening day for pantomime, and there was the chance that it might be too early for people to be in the real pantomime spirit. Despite this, Southend gave them a fine welcome and the audience revelled in the frivolities of Sandy's version of this most popular of fairy stories.

With the show moving smoothly and improving with each performance, they all looked forward to the London opening the following week. However, the coming Saturday performance was rather worrying. In booking Alec Ross for one of the broker's men and Frank Lorden for the Baron, Sandy had engaged two excellent performers, but he had been warned that Saturday was Frank's 'drinking day' (he never touched alcohol during the week). As an insurance Sandy asked Alec to learn the Baron's part. About half an hour before the Saturday matinee was due to begin, Sandy received the news that Frank had just come in and was 'incapable of going on'. Going to his dressing-room Sandy found him almost asleep in his chair. Calling his manager Sandy said, 'What a blessing we've got Alec standing by to play the Baron.' But when he went to Alec's dressing-room Alec himself was 'out to the wide'. It transpired that they'd both been out together on a drinking session. The cast managed to scramble through the matinee without them and Sandy allowed them to sleep it off. About a half hour before the start of the evening performance, Sandy went to Frank's dressing-room, and found him made-up, ready to go on. Sandy told him, 'You're not fit to go on, Frank.'

Frank replied, 'If I was fit enough to go on for the bloody matinee, I am fit enough to go on tonight.' Sandy said, 'You didn't go on for the bloody matinee and you're not going on tonight either!' Alec had also got himself ready, but they were both 'excused' from performing that night and, as in the matinee, they managed without them. They both pleaded with Sandy to overlook it, and giving their solemn promise that it would not happen again, the matter was dropped; and it never did happen again. Sandy had quite a few experiences like this and realised that there is a special providence that

looks after drunks and children, and that the stage is full of children of
mature age.

When they arrived at Shepherds Bush, Sandy was delighted to hear that
bookings were heavy. They had a rapturous reception at the first show from
a packed audience in which the children outnumbered the adults by about
three to one. Unfortunately there was a disaster during the scene that closed
the first half. The Dawson's Canary Choir was doing splendidly and the
audience loved them; the canaries were warbling away beautifully right
to their finale, during which the cue was given to start up the Crystal Fairy
Fountains. But instead of the fountains dancing up and down, a great
stream of water gushed out and ran right across the stage and down into the
orchestra pit. It made so much noise that the singing of the canaries could
not be heard at all, and the curtain was hastily dropped for the intermission.
It was discovered that the water jets were damaged and had not been
properly checked, probably because they had worked so well at Southend
the previous week. The apparatus had to be hastily repaired and the stage
hurriedly mopped up, with profuse apologies to the music director and his
musicians, who had carried on bravely despite the deluge. The second half
of the programme ran smoothly much to Sandy's relief. The theatrical
and national newspapers described the show as being one of the finest
companies seen in suburban pantomime. This opinion was also shared by
the public, and within a few days the theatre was completely booked out
for the entire two weeks. Stoll's hurriedly rescheduled all their booking
arrangements in order to retain the show for a further week before going to
Hackney for the next fortnight.

Sandy knew that he now had a winner in putting on children's pantomime, and that his name on a bill was enough to bring the customers to the
theatre. A fact that was also appreciated by Moss Empires who stepped in
smartly with a very handsome offer to put on the same show the following
season at the Empire, Sheffield, and then at the Leeds Empire.

Sandy had now become one of the biggest box-office attractions of the
day and his success in radio, records, music hall and pantomime ensured
that his name on the bill meant packed houses. It was the Julian Wylie
office who made the next big offer for him to play in their pantomime *Puss
in Boots* at the Theatre Royal, Birmingham, for the 1935–6 season that was
to be presented by Tom Arnold. From the financial point of view it was
tempting, and it also meant that Sandy wouldn't have the responsibility of
putting on the show, but he was dubious as to his suitability for this particular theatre. He told George Black, who also had an interest in the show,
that he thought it could be a mistake.

'The Royal isn't my cup of tea,' he said. 'I've worked the Alec several
times and the audience there is friendly. The Royal is different, the people
are more reserved, stuffy, in fact; I'd die a death there.'

Black replied, 'Sandy you're absolutely wrong. The Royal isn't a
cathedral, its a theatre. I want you to work there exactly as you worked in
the Alec.'

Glamour and gruffness. The two sides of Sandy's dame in Goldilocks *at the Theatre Royal, Bath, 1961.*

'Can I go out front and gag with the kids as I did at the Alec?' queried Sandy.

'That's exactly what I want you to do, just that, work in your usual way, do just as you like,' said Black.

Sandy signed the contract and did as Black advised. The result was a resounding success and they played three times daily for a record run.

The Theatre Royal, Birmingham, was one of the great pantomime theatres with a tradition going back a long way. Two very fine pantomime artists, Wee Georgie Wood and Clarkson Rose, had made a big name there, and strangely enough, for this particular season, they were starring at the Alexandra for Leon Salberg, where Sandy had been such a huge success; so it was a fair 'exchange'. Birmingham was very rich in pantomime that season: the Prince of Wales Theatre had an all-star cast which included the Houston Sisters (Renee and Billie) and the superb West End Comedian, Douglas Byng. There was indeed tremendous competition between the three theatres, but despite the strong opposition *Puss in Boots* more than held its own. In fact the critic of the influential *Birmingham Weekly* wrote: 'I have never heard a more sincere compliment to an artist than paid by Leon Salberg, when he said that if anyone could hit us this year it would be Sandy Powell.'

Rehearsals at which both Tom Arnold and George Black officiated, were hectic but great fun because the cast was a very happy crowd and Sandy commented on this to Black, who replied, 'You set the tempo on the first day; you were the first to arrive at rehearsal, most of them are used to seeing stars arrive hours late and make a big entrance, or send word they wouldn't be in until the afternoon. You've been different and that is why we are going to have a happy show.'

Sandy was reminded of the 'Edelsten affair' one day when he was sitting in the stalls with the producer watching the other artists running through their material. Comedian Fred Gwyn was doing a solo spot as the dame and was getting big laughs from the artists, stage hands and staff. Arnold turned to Sandy and said, 'Do you want this dame out Sandy?'

Sandy replied, 'What do you mean "out"? He's great, one of the best dames I've seen, he'll tear them to pieces.'

'That's the point,' said Arnold, 'many top-of-the-bill comics wouldn't want to work with this fellow, he gets too many laughs.'

Although Sandy had learnt about this sort of ruthlessness in his first show working with George Hyams, and also when Ernest Edelsten interviewed him, he couldn't understand this kind of attitude, and still doesn't. As far as he is concerned, the more laughs there are the better it is for the show. It is this altruistic attitude that has made Sandy the beloved and esteemed member of the theatre that he is.

Up to this time Sandy never wore glasses on the stage, but sometimes there were publicity pictures of him wearing them, so at George Black's suggestion he started to wear glasses on stage no matter what part he played. He soon started using them for gags and developed quite a few of them over the years; the best-remembered one being that when he wanted to examine an object more closely, he lifted the spectacles to his eyebrows and then brought the object right up close to his naked eyes. This is an original gag which has gone into the repertoire of comedians who came after him. For example, Eric Morecambe uses it these days to great effect.

Puss in Boots was billed as being staged and devised by Tom Arnold and it was a magnificent production, with eighteen colourful scenes using almost every pantomime gimmick. Arnold modelled the scenario from the book by the brilliant comedian-author Marriott Edgar (of *Albert and the Lion* and *Sam Pick Up Thy Musket* fame), and it was a novel adaptation of the *Puss in Boots* fable. Sandy was the Miller's assistant who helped Colin the hero, delightfully played by the popular broadcasting star Eve Becke, in various adventures culminating in the hero gaining the kingdom. The cat, a very important part, was played by Laurie Mellin. Marjorie Lotinga was a sprightly Princess to whom the hero lost his heart; the unctuous dame was played with great gusto by comedian Fred Gwyn; the Millers were the fine dancers De Haven and Page and the famous variety act 'Hibbert, Bird and La Rue' featured their sensational Octopus Dance. Pepino's Circus with dogs, monkeys, horses and ponies gave great enjoyment to the children, who were also excited by the thrilling acrobatics of the Seven Royal Hindustans and the amazing Kirby Flying Ballet. The large number of children as fairies and the precision dancing of the Sherman Fisher Girls made it a pantomime to remember.

It is interesting to record as a sign of the times the report by the theatrical critic of the national newspaper with the largest circulation, *The News of the World*. He wrote in the issue dated 23rd February 1936:

Today pantomime survives in London at the Lyceum alone. In the provinces it is different, as pantomime in the big cities remains an obstinate and obdurate success. Last week I saw *Puss in Boots* at Birmingham's Theatre Royal and marvelled at the business. Yet why marvel? The production which will remain for another month at least, suffers nothing in comparison with West End standards and its gay and gifted company are ideally cast. The funmaker in chief, Sandy Powell, is undoubtedly one of the greatest pantomime artists of the day. He has the happy knack of quickly getting on to terms of intimacy with the children, and it is not long before his every entry is hailed with yells of welcome from every part of the house.

Despite working twice daily at 2 p.m. and 7 p.m., Sandy devoted a great deal of time and thought into putting to good use the enthusiasm of his young fans, and in December 1935 he started the 'Sandy Powell Gang'. Leaflets were printed in which there was a letter from Sandy. It was addressed to 'My Dear Kiddies' and it asked them to join his 'Gang of Good Deed Workers'. All the children had to do was to go along to the Theatre Royal in New Street and purchase from the booking office a Sandy Powell badge for one penny which automatically enrolled them as members of the gang, provided they obeyed the rules. The money received from the sale of badges and sales of his photograph in the theatre was to be divided without any deductions whatever, equally between the *Birmingham Mail* Christmas Tree Fund and the *Evening Despatch* Dog-Licences Fund. The leaflet also stated that there were to be a series of special Saturday morning concerts for gang members and that admission would be free. The Sandy Powell Gang Rules were as follows:

Rule 1:   Obedience to parents and guardians at all times.
Rule 2:   Kindness to animals always.
Rule 3:   Always speak the truth.
Rule 4:   To help and assist the blind, the infirmed and the aged in crossing roads, in boarding trams or buses and so forth.
Rule 5:   To share your joys and pleasures with other kiddies.
Rule 6:   Whenever you meet the Chief Gangster, that is myself, you are to fold your arms, walk straight up and say in a loud voice 'Hello Sandy'.

Any badge-wearing member failing to fulfil the last rule will be fined one penny, the proceeds to go to the joint charities.

It was a highly imaginative and worthwhile scheme and caught on like wildfire. The box office was besieged by eager applicants at the end of every performance and when Sandy came down from the stage still dressed in his working clothes to personally help in the sale of his photographs, which he gladly autographed, they clamoured for them. The result was a large sum of money for local charities. Sandy Powell Gangs were set up when working in a resident show in other provincial cities and membership rose to well over seventy-five thousand. In the process many thousands of pounds were raised for charitable causes.

The pantomime *Puss in Boots* and Sandy's Gang aroused the interest of a distinguished French journalist who used them as the basis of a series of articles for a magazine on the traditional English pantomime, which caused a great deal of interest on the Continent.

Sandy's great popularity with the children was recognised when he was asked to do a series in a popular children's comic, *Film Fun*. It was a great success.

The night before the show closed Sandy organised a Pantomime Ball at Tony's Ballroom. A tremendous crowd turned up which included most of the actors and actresses working in Birmingham as well as the general public. Sandy and his family were there and very busy on the various raffles and other money-raising devices for charity. The guests included Eve Becke and the entire company from the Royal, Renee and Billy Houston with Douglas Byng and the rest of the cast from the Prince of Wales, Clarkson Rose and Wee Georgie Wood from the Alexander and the Western Brothers from the Hippodrome music hall. The entire proceeds were given to Brinsworth, the home for old performers in Twickenham, Middlesex, where they could live out their last years and which was main-tained and looked after by the profession.

The next day was the matinee, and the final performance in the evening.

Another dame from Sandy's repertoire of characters. Seen here in Bunny Baron's Robinson Crusoe *at the White Rock, Hastings, 1962.*

It was the end of a most successful run, which incidentally was the longest in the Theatre Royal's long pantomime history.

After the show Sandy had one of the most hectic weekends of his life, starting with the clearing-up after the pantomime and then having to make the journey to Coventry where his *Road Show* was due on the Monday. He and the company rehearsed all through Sunday and into the small hours of Monday. After a short sleep they had to rehearse again with the pit orchestra and make the final preparations for a week's variety before setting out for another tour of the music halls. This was what usually happened to variety artists that worked pantomime seasons: the change from one to the other was generally a hectic rush.

A few weeks after the opening of the pantomime in Birmingham, Tom Arnold told Sandy that he wanted him to appear at the Empire, Liverpool, for him the following season. 'Sorry,' said Sandy, 'I'm afraid that you have left it too late. Mike [Mike Lyon, Sandy's agent] told me that as he hadn't heard from you he has booked me with Wylie & Tate for their show here next Christmas.'

'We will see about that,' commented Arnold. A few months later Arnold got in touch with Sandy and said, 'I told you that you would be working for me next season.'

'Oh no I'm not,' protested Sandy.

'Oh yes you are,' replied Arnold. 'You really are working for me Sandy. Mind you I've had to do it the hard way and buy out Wylie & Tate to get you on my books.' Arnold had taken over Wylie & Tate, and in doing so Sandy's contract with that firm. So now Sandy was working personally for Tom Arnold. As the Empire, Liverpool, was one of Sandy's favourite theatres he was happy with the arrangement.

The cast at Liverpool was almost the same as at Birmingham, except that Nita Croft took over from Eve Becke and Barbara Bartle was the Princess. Immediately after the opening of the show Tom Arnold booked Sandy for the Palace, Manchester, for the following season to play in a very spectacular production of *Cinderella*.

Sandy was Buttons and was supported by an all-star cast which included the famous West End comedian Freddie Forbes playing Lobelia, one of the Ugly Sisters, Jean Adrienne who had been leading lady in many big London shows, as Prince Charming. Iris March who had recently appeared in one of Sandy's films, played Cinderella, and the Australian actress Clarice Hardwicke as Dandini made her first provincial appearance after a great success in the role at the Theatre Royal, Drury Lane. Roy Jeffries was Baron Everbroke, Lulu the celebrated 'Human Horse' and the sensational adagio act 'Romance in Porcelain' was featured with the Ganjou Brothers and Juanita.

The production was in the true Tom Arnold style with revolving stage constructed to facilitate quick changes of the lavish scenes. The pantomime played to packed houses and with heavy advance bookings, a record run was confidently expected. Sandy recalls the 'largest theatre party in the world' taking place at the end of January; the Metropolitan Vickers Electrical Company booked over twelve thousand seats comprising four consecutive nights and a matinee performance for their night staff. The Co-operative Society also booked the theatre completely for two nights and the merchandise firms of Rylands and Lewis stores each had a single-night booking. The theatre management naturally sought and encouraged this social tendency. Sandy with his experience at the 'Alec' in Birmingham was able to introduce many of the gags and stunts which he had used so successfully previously. 'Sandy's Gang' and other charitable endeavours kept him busy during his spare time, but he was overdoing things and began to feel the strain. His doctor ordered him a complete rest, but he struggled on until he had to see a specialist, who warned him that unless he gave up work he would have a complete breakdown. Sandy's illness was kept a secret from the company and the public. Although it was becoming obvious that he was not fit there were many secret telephone calls, medical and managerial conferences, and finally the search to find a substitute for him. The show had three more weeks to run and secrecy was necessary because thousands of pounds of advance bookings had been made.

Eventually Sandy's friend Will Fyffe agreed to take over. Tom Arnold after difficult negotiations was able to find alternative top of the bills for the theatres at which Will Fyffe was already booked to appear, so Sandy was able to leave the cast. The members of the company were astonished when they found out one Saturday night that Sandy was leaving the show, but readily agreed to sacrifice their Sunday off to rehearse with Will Fyffe. Sandy himself was relieved that all was well and he left for the South of France for a complete rest and a holiday that was his first for many years.

The 1938–9 pantomime season was missed because of heavy advance bookings for his *Road Show*. Then came the outbreak of the Second World War and after the initial shock of having to adjust to wartime conditions, the theatres carried on the best they could. The provincial theatres did well and Bert Montague engaged Sandy to appear for him in *Babes in the Wood* at the New Coventry Hippodrome, and, knowing that Sandy was a draw in Coventry, the offer was a salary plus a percentage of the takings.

Sandy's name on the bill was the cue for good business and the public thronged to the booking office. On the first Saturday night Bert Montague went to Sandy's dressing-room to pay him for the first week's work. He pulled out an enormous wad of pound notes and slowly and deliberately counted them on to the dressing-room table as if each note he put down caused him some degree of pain. He counted 'one, two, three' and so on until he had reached one hundred. He hesitated and looked Sandy right in the eye, sighed deeply and continued counting. 'One hundred and one, one hundred and two' and so on to 'two hundred', then hesitated again sighed even more deeply and went on in this way until the total had reached just under four hundred pounds. Bert straightened up and said, 'There you are Sandy, not a bad week's work.' But his style of paying out was just an elaborate piece of fun.

For the season of 1940–1 Sandy decided to take out his own production of *Cinderella* again, and his agent Mike Lyon booked him Stoll dates; two weeks at the Chiswick Empire followed by another two weeks at the Wood Green Empire. At the time these dates were booked, things were quiet, a period which became known as the 'Phoney War'. But, after the fall of France, bombing attacks on Britain began in earnest, school children were hurriedly evacuated from London and in September the capital sustained great damage in a very heavy raid. It was decided to carry on if possible and the show opened on Boxing Day, as usual. Performances took place at 2 p.m. and 6 p.m. and in these circumstances business was not too bad. It was a few days later that a severe incendiary bombing on central London came, and all performances were cancelled. They opened a fortnight later at the Wood Green Empire as scheduled but the same thing happened; no sooner did the show begin than they had to close almost immediately because of the bombing. Sandy was amusingly referred to as being the 'best opener and closer of theatres in the business'.

It was with typical war-time optimism that Moss Empires booked Sandy's *Cinderella* for the 1941–2 season, two weeks at Finsbury Park Empire, in North London. Some weeks prior to this date, Sandy received a call from his agent to meet Leslie Grade, who with his brother Lew (now Sir Lew Grade) and his other brother Bernard Delfont (now Sir Bernard Delfont) were big agents. Sandy was surprised to see Leslie wearing his 'props', his Royal Air Force uniform. Although Leslie was in the R.A.F. he carried on agency work in his spare time and put on big shows for the forces at Hendon Aerodrome. He said, 'Sandy, I have always admired your work and I would like my name coupled with yours.'

Sandy replied, 'In what way?'

Grade said, 'Let me run your pantomime because I would like the bill to read "Sandy Powell and Leslie Grade presents Cinderella".'

'On what arrangement?' asked Sandy. Grade replied, 'I would like to take over your bill and pay you a guarantee of three hundred pounds a week plus a percentage, and in addition I will pay you a hundred pounds a week for the hire of the production, scenery and costumes. I will also pay all your artists, and if I want to put in any extra artists that will be my financial responsibility.' This sounded good to Sandy, a guarantee of four hundred pounds a week, plus a percentage of the takings and the fact that he was relieved of all worry of running the show, made it an attractive proposition. This proved successful and arrangements were later made for their cooperation in variety.

The show opened to excellent business at Finsbury Park and advance bookings were good. At this time there were only two pantomimes open in London: Sandy's and the other at the Golders Green Hippodrome. A couple of days later Sandy was shocked when he was told by Mike Lyon that Val Parnell of Moss Empires had been in to see the show and was quite adamant that an extra act had to be put in to strengthen the bill for the second week. At Mike's suggestion 'Harry Lester and His Hayseeds' was to be that act. According to Harry Lester he was thunderstruck at the idea of his Hayseeds Cowboy Band performing in pantomime, but Mike Lyon told him to go in and see Sandy, which he did on the following night. Lester said that Sandy threw up his hands in disgust at being forced to take the act, and said that he did not care what Harry Lester had to show, that it would not make any difference as advance bookings indicated that they would have capacity business without them. Lester's band had been one of the most popular headline acts in the business, but many of his men had been called up for the services and he had disbanded in consequence. In September 1941 he had just finished a season in Jack Taylor's show at the South Pier, Blackpool and had heard that 'Goofus', an important member of his band had been discharged from the Home Guard, so he decided to revive the Hayseeds' act again. They rehearsed in Blackpool and played a couple of 'frees' for practice. The six-handed act which included Babs, Harry's talented wife, went across well when they played a string of variety dates around the country. Engagements then slowed down and Harry went to London to see some big agents, who were immediately interested, but when getting on the telephone to Moss Empires they were told, 'Not interested in Harry Lester and his Hayseeds'. At that the agents dropped them like a piece of hot coal.

In desperation Harry went to Mike Lyon, who listened to his story, looked at the publicity pictures of the act and read the glowing newspaper reports of their recent tour. Harry told him frankly about Moss Empires, rejection, but undeterred Lyon only said, 'Good acts are scarce and they cannot afford to ignore one.' He pulled a few strings and got them the trial week booking with Sandy.

Harry was given ten minutes in the palace ball scene in Sandy's panto-mime. He says that he will never forget the look of utter amazement on Sandy's face when the Hayseeds galloped into the palace scene shouting, 'We have come to entertain the Prince!' To see a gang of cowboys and hillbillies break in on what was a traditional medieval setting was equally astonishing to the audience. To the Hayseeds it was the hit of their career when their version of 'We'll Be Coming Round the Mountain' held up the ball for some minutes, and the attitude of the audience was 'forget the ball, we want more of the Hayseeds!' Harry says that even to this day he doesn't know what Sandy thought about it all, but whatever it did, it certainly provided the right opportunity for the triumphant return of the Hayseeds, and, as Mike Lyon said, they couldn't be ignored after that hit. Harry Lester says that he later learnt it was the policy of Moss Empires to force show proprietors to take extra acts unnecessarily in order to embarrass them. In this case they couldn't ignore the money-making potential of the Hayseeds and they were back on the Moss tour again. It was Miss Cissie Williams, Moss's booking manager, who later got them into the Royal Performance.

Sandy and Harry Lester became good friends after this episode, and the Hayseeds later worked in Sandy's road shows. Both Harry's wife Babs and

The King smiles benignly. Puss in Boots *at the New Theatre, Cardiff, 1968.*

his son Bob played in Sandy's pantomimes.

The year after the war during the season 1946–7, Sandy worked in *Red Riding Hood*, a Wylie & Tate production staged in Britain's largest theatre, the Opera House, Blackpoool. It was a season which proved to be most distressing for Sandy as his wife had recently died. He asked his agent to get him released from his contract, but he was advised to force himself to work in order to overcome his depression. He was greatly helped by George Bolton, a member of the cast with whom he had worked some years previously in Coventry. George now proved his friendship by shielding Sandy at rehearsals. Whenever they were called on stage to rehearse their particular episodes, he would call out 'Mr Producer, to save time Mr Powell and I will rehearse this ourselves – O.K.?' The understanding producer consented and thus saved Sandy the possibility of making errors in front of the whole cast. It gave him the chance to settle down and he was ever grateful for the kindness and understanding of his fellow pros.

Bob Lester, played the part of the Wolf, and Sandy remembers a girl playing the part of Gretchen; a part specially written in so that she could do her impersonations act. He was sure she had a good future ahead of her and this she certainly did. Her name was Beryl Reid, who many years later became an international star of stage, films and television.

The North country impresario Jack Taylor approached Mike Lyon about Sandy doing pantomime for him: three weeks at the Theatre Royal, Bolton, to be followed by two weeks at the Empire, Sunderland. Lyon and Taylor were not fond of each other and Mike rubbed his hands at the prospect of getting the last ounce of blood from the Taylor stone. He told Sandy: 'As Jack has asked for you specially, I'm going to get you a real contract – big guaranteed salary plus percentage, top billing, number-one dressing-room – the lot!' Taylor signed the tough contract as he wanted Sandy in his show. A few weeks later, however, he telephoned Sandy and said, 'I've got a chance to book Josef Locke for the panto. You know Joe is a bighead, he wants top billing, number-one dressing-room and all that, he knows he's a big draw, but I can't give him anything like that because of your contract. Will you help me in this, Sandy?'

'As far as I am concerned, Jack, you can put my name on the back of the bill, and as long as the dressing-room is within walking distance of the theatre it will suit me; give him what he wants if he wants it that badly.'

'Thanks,' said Taylor, 'I hoped that you'd be helpful, but I didn't know you were that keen on Joe.'

'I'm not, as far as he is concerned personally,' replied Sandy, 'but he'll be working for me as I am on shares, the more people he draws in, the more he will be earning for me.'

Josef Locke the Irish tenor was one of the biggest draw cards in the business at that time, and as soon as his name was seen on the bill with Sandy's, the three weeks season with three performances daily produced full houses at each performance at Bolton and at the Sunderland Empire. Josef Locke was a fine singer and a great showman, just the personality that music hall audiences loved, but he was not an easy man to work with; he had an odd sense of humour.

Sandy, who was keen on soccer, had a radio and wanted to listen to a broadcast of a first-division game of some importance between the famous London side Tottenham Hotspur and the local team Sunderland F.C. Sandy said, 'Joe, Sunderland are playing the Spurs this afternoon while we are working the matinee. They are crackers on football up here and if you are on stage and Sunderland score I'll give you the tip from the wings and you tell them; it will get you a big round of applause for nothing. If it happens while I'm on stage you can do the same for me.'

'A great idea,' said Joe. The first action happened when Sandy was on stage and he saw Joe in the wings holding up two fingers and mouthing the word 'Sunderland' and then making a circle with his first finger and thumb saying 'Spurs nil.' Sandy got the message, stepped out of character and said 'Ladies and Gentlemen, I have some news which I think will please you. The news from Roker Park is that Sunderland are leading Spurs by two goals to nil.' The audience went raving mad and nearly lifted off the roof with their cheers. Sandy finished his spot to tremendous applause. A little while later Joe made an entrance, walked straight down to the footlights and said 'Ladies and Gentlemen, I think you ought to know that when Sandy Powell told you that Sunderland were two up, he was kidding, actually the Spurs are leading by two goals to nothing.' When Sandy made his next entrance the audience gave him a very rough ride, almost the 'bird', but of course he couldn't tell them the truth.

The following year Sandy had the unique experience of working in two different pantomimes in two different towns for two different managements. This extraordinary state of affairs came about in the following way. After playing an eight-week season in *Mother Goose* at the Grand, Doncaster, Sandy drove back to London arriving home early on the Sunday morning. He hadn't been in bed very long before the telephone rang. It was Mike Lyon to ask whether he had enjoyed Doncaster. 'It was a bit hectic, I can do with a rest,' replied Sandy.

'Too bad,' said Mike, 'I've had an urgent call from Birmingham, Frankie Howard in *Babes in the Wood* has been taken suddenly ill and they are relying on you to deputise. You are on tomorrow for the matinee. Jimmy Wheeler is going up with you, so you can sort something out between you on the way. A car will collect you at eight in the morning.' They went off in the morning as arranged, did some gags and odd bits and pieces to get them through the matinee and for the evening show Sandy did his popular sketch 'Going to the Pictures', while Jimmy Wheeler, a fine comedian who had just scored a big success at the London Palladium did his new music-hall act. Both Sandy and Jimmy had played *Babes in the Wood* before and it didn't take them long to drop into the routine again.

Two more pantomime roles were added to Sandy's repertoire when he played the Queen in *Jack and Jill* at the Royal, Bath, and *Little Miss Muffet* also at the same theatre a year later, and then the following year at the Lyceum, Newport. The productions were by Frank Maddox.

After an evening performance at Newport, he came out of the theatre with Frank Maddox and a friend, who was a doctor. In stepping off the pavement to cross the road, Sandy felt that he had done something to his ankle. The pain was excruciating and the doctor insisted that they got him to hospital, where his foot was put in plaster and he was taken back to his hotel. When Frank Maddox visited him the next morning and asked how he felt and what could they do about the show, Sandy replied, 'My toe is broken and I must not put any weight on my leg, but otherwise, I feel fine!'

Frank said 'If I got a wheel chair and got one of the girls to push you on for your entrances, do you think you could manage?'

'Let's try it,' said Sandy, and they did this for the Friday night performance and the two shows on the Saturday. So, for the first time in the history of pantomime, the Queen made her entrances wheeled on in a bath-chair! Sandy enjoyed himself and the audience being more than sympathetic, was exceedingly generous in its applause. However, the toe took eight weeks to mend and, since he couldn't work dates in a wheelchair, they had to be cancelled.

When his years started to advance, Sandy realised the time had come to relinquish the roles of Buttons and Simple Simon which had taken him to the top in this field. He then started to develop the other classic role in pantomime, the Dame. Over the years he had worked with the greatest, pantomime actors, so he started with some advantage, and with the same thoroughness that he had applied to his previous roles: he became, as Bunny Baron insists, 'the best Dame in the business'. Bunny was pleased when Sandy agreed to play Dame in *Robinson Crusoe* at the White Rock, Hastings, and the following year at Weston Super Mare. Bunny Baron had been in the business since a boy and played most of the famous 'boy' parts with great stars like Seymour Hicks and Ellaline Terris, then played in repertory as an actor. He now enjoys telling about the time in 1935 when he lived at 169 Dudden Hill Lane in Neasden, Middlesex, and Sandy lived at 173. Bunny had run into a rough patch, for work and money were very scarce at that time. He says that he used to watch for Sandy to come out of his house so that he could approach him about the possibility of work, but he was never able to pluck up the courage. In later years they became firm friends, and they both laugh at the irony of Bunny the nervous, penniless neighbour almost thirty years later engaging Sandy to work in his pantomime!

Coming up to the seventies Sandy played other parts including that of the King in *Puss in Boots* with his wife Kay playing the role of Queen. Even now, there is still the same wonderful rapport between the children and Sandy whatever part he plays: for the magic of Sandy Powell and the magic of pantomime are inseparable.

3

Over the Air

URING the run of Julian Wylie's *Blackpool Follies* in the summer of 1928, wireless producer Victor Smythe asked Sandy to broadcast his famous sketch 'The Lost Policeman'. This posed a problem because at that time there was a good deal of controversy within the profession about the wisdom of artistes going on the air. The Variety Artists Federation had emphatically expressed the opinion that it was detrimental to the best interests of artists to broadcast. Sandy, however, was of the opinion that the advertising value of broadcasting could be a good thing for variety, and he became a pioneer in this medium. He said 'yes' to Victor Smythe and so, for the first time, he went on the air.

The studio was a small room in the Blackpool Tower building and the working conditions could hardly be described as 'luxurious'. The performance was of course 'live' since it was long before the days of recorded programmes.

'The Lost Policeman' was a good choice for Sandy's first broadcast. He had introduced it to music-hall audiences some years before and it was a well-established favourite. The sketch was a dialogue between a cheeky young boy and Sandy as the Policeman, with the boy getting the better of most of the exchanges between them. The lines delivered with a slight Northern accent were not only appealing, but very distinctive. The session was so successful that he was asked to go to London to broadcast from the Savoy Hill Studio. This time he did a variety act which he included a monologue 'Pity the Goldfish', cracked some gags and finished with a song. This went over so well with the listening public as well as the BBC that during the next few months it developed into a regular feature which went out on the air every few weeks. Two- and three-handed sketches were interpolated with songs and gags, a formula that proved very successful. Soon the show was extended into a full hour revue called *Sandy's Hour*, this being the very first time that a variety programme was broadcast.

Eventually he went on the air once a month, and his was the first regular variety show on wireless. Each programme was a mixture of sketches, songs and jokes, done 'live' twice a week. This of course meant that Sandy's variety bookings schedule had to be re-arranged to fit it all in. A further and increasingly popular run of shows followed which were called by various names: *Pages from Sandy's Album, More Pages from Sandy's Album*, and *Sandy Powell's Road Show*.

In the meantime Sandy carried on correspondence with George Black in which he emphasised that his broadcasts were helpful to variety, and some months after Sandy's first broadcast – on 22nd October 1928, the act of Van and Schenk, the American comedians was broadcast from the stage of the London Palladium, a theatre belonging to one of many management who had barred acts from working on the wireless.

One of the greatest catch-phrases of all time came into being during one of the *Sandy's Hour* broadcasts, and it happened quite by accident. Over the years many garbled versions of this episode have been told, but this is the first true version as related by Sandy himself. He was broadcasting a sketch called 'Sandy at the North Pole'. The announcer started the proceedings.

Voice: Before the weather forecast, I am sure you will all be pleased to know that Sandy Powell, who was reported in all the papers as missing, is safe at the North Pole. Fortunately he took with him a wireless transmission set and in a few moments we are going to relay him. He will give you his own story direct from the North Pole. (Atmospheric noises etc.)

Sandy: Hello, hello, is that London? Sandy speaking, not Bandy – Sandy. I'm speaking from the North Pole. The North Pole not the May Pole. I arrived quite safe and am quite well except for a few chilblains and a frozen diary. Yes, here I am, and let me tell you that it was harder to find than the winner of the Lincoln handicap. Can you hear me? Will you be able to relay what I'm saying please? I would like my mother to know that I've found the North Pole and that I'm safe and sound. I wouldn't trouble you only I haven't found the post office yet. Hello, will Mrs Brown of 17 Bloaters Row go immediately to the Prince of Wales and fetch my mother out of the saloon bar? Tell her to leave her bread and milk and come and listen to her son Sandy speaking from the North Pole. I left Chorlton-cum-Hardy four years ago come Friday. I was given the freedom of the city before leaving. I don't think anyone ever expected me to get back, and I know it was the wife's idea that I went. Can you hear me Mother?

At this moment Sandy accidentally dropped his script on the floor of the studio, and while picking up the pages he kept things going by ad-libbing; anything that came into his head. During this he repeated the phrase 'Can you Hear Me Mother?' many times not thinking of it as a particularly funny line, but an appropriate one while he gathered the pages together. Having got over that little spot of bother, they carried on normally, and the matter was soon forgotten, because the line had been written-in as a line of dialogue, and was repeated a few times later because atmospheric noises in the background were apparently causing reception difficulties. It was not planned or intended as a catch-phrase line.

However, a couple of days later at the Monday morning band call, the music rehearsal with the Coventry Hippodrome pit orchestra, the theatre manager said to Sandy, 'Good show on Saturday night, that new catch-

The Lost Policeman – this was Sandy's first sketch to be broadcast by radio, 1928.

phrase of yours is a real winner, its buzzing all round Coventry.'

'What catch-phrase?' queried Sandy.

The manager replied, 'Are you kidding? I mean that funny line you said on the air: "Can you hear me, Mother?" Everybody's talking about it. I bet that if you used it as an entrance line tonight, you'll get a big round of applause.'

Sandy took his advice and when he came on stage, said, 'Can you hear me, Mother?' and it was greeted, as the manager had predicted, with a burst of loud and prolonged applause. Ever since that night, it has been his opening line at every performance.

Perhaps most amazing of all is the fact that its popularity continued right through the years and is still remembered by audiences not only in Great Britain, but in New Zealand, South Africa and other parts of the world. During the Second World War when Sandy went to Naples for E.N.S.A. (the organisation that arranged entertainments for the troops), he'd hardly got off the ship when soldiers called out to him 'Can you hear me, Mother?' Touring South Africa and New Zealand, it was quite commonplace for people to come up and say, 'Can you hear me, Mother?' in the street.

Flying from South Africa *en route* to New Zealand during their 1970 tour, Sandy changed planes at Perth in Western Australia and a customs official greeted him with the words 'Well, look who's here, it's the "Can you hear me, Mother?" man, Sandy Powell!'

Puzzled, Sandy replied, 'I don't understand this, how do you know me?'

'We all know your voice over here, your records are played on the radio every Saturday morning. "Sandy the Dentist" and "Sandy Joins the Nudists" are my great favourites.' It was amazing that he was so easily recognised by records made nearly forty years previously.

Arthur Le Clair who wrote the famous catch-phrase was Sandy's main scriptwriter at that time, and was naturally highly delighted (and surprised) at its success. But further attempts to repeat the success with other catch-phrases came to naught. Similar lines like 'I wish I had as many shillings' and 'I've seen this coming for a long time' were deliberately contrived and planted in other sketches, but although getting a big laugh at the time, they never really caught on and were soon forgotten. 'Can you Hear Me Mother?' was the first catch-phrase on the air that really clicked, and even today, if he doesn't include the famous line, he gets many letters, asking why!

It is interesting to note that Robb Wilton's 'The day the War broke out', and Arthur Askey's 'I thank you' were also accidents that were never intended as catch-phrases.

An amusing incident remembered by Sandy happened when he was working at the Liverpool Empire with his *Road Show*. As was usual at the big-capacity Moss Empire theatres, the bill was augmented by a big-name act. It was a star from America working on this bill for the purpose of getting the feel of an English audience before opening in London the following week. The house manager took him to Sandy's dressing-room and said, 'Meet Sandy Powell, one of our country's biggest stars.' Sandy sensed that the American didn't know him (as a matter of fact he didn't know the American either) and he was surprised when he said politely, 'Happy to meet you, Mr Powell. Of course I've heard all about you, you're famous in my country.'

'That's strange,' replied Sandy, 'I've never worked there.'

'Maybe not,' said the American, 'but, it's that catch-phrase of yours, it's cute, everybody in America knows it – "How's your Father"!'

BBC television transmissions started in a small way at No. 16 Portland Place, in London's West End, and Sandy was the first to be invited to bring his company, and measure their talents in a strange new medium. The props were makeshift, and the Easter-egg shaped microphone was always in view. Working in front of a simple, painted backcloth; makeup, lighting and camera positions presented problems to be overcome by 'the boys in the back room'. It wasn't easy for Sandy and his artists either, but it was a memorable occasion, and he is proud that not only was he a pioneer in 'Sound' on the Wireless, but also in 'Vision' on television.

It was at Sandy's suggestion that George Black accepted the idea of advertising that stars of radio were working his theatres, and some other managements followed this lead. Soon stars of radio were topping the bills and during the thirties and onwards they provided the biggest attractions in music hall; a move that turned an established music-hall tradition upside down.

Previously one only reached stardom after a lengthy and laborious apprenticeship of working around, learning the business by a hard and sometimes very painful process. Now, almost at a stroke, stars of radio, without any music-hall background and training, became headliners on the halls and attracted big audiences. The public's desire to see their great radio and recording favourites 'in the flesh' overcame any of the stars' shortcomings as stage performers. And this perhaps was the moment when gimmicks took over as a substitute for stage technique and talent that could only be learnt by a long apprenticeship and working experience. It was the start of the 'press-button' road to fame and fortune.

Radio also provided an opportunity for experienced performers in other fields, such as concert party, musical comedy, legitimate actors and band-leaders. Arthur Askey and Richard Murdoch were a typical example of this new phenomena. 'Big-hearted Arthur' was a concert-party artist who also worked dinners, Masonic's, private parties and cabaret. Richard Murdoch was a musical-comedy man, a dancer and comedian, and while both did very well in their respective fields, real fame didn't come to them until they went on the air in a radio show called *Band Wagon*: it was an enormous success and became the first radio series, with each show being an instalment of a continuing story at a set location – unlike Sandy's regular variety shows which were unrelated to each other.

Sandy's radio shows continued to be extremely popular, and were being broadcast from the studio and also direct from theatres. However, there were still managements and artists who were scared of this increasingly popular medium. Eric Maschwitz, BBC director of Light Entertainment wrote in 1935 in the theatrical paper *The Era*:

In the South of England there are music halls we should like to broadcast from regularly, but the managements are not prepared to cooperate with us – so far. The notion that relays are bad for business still holds good in some Southern quarters. The vast majority of present day variety stars – Elsie Carlisle, Les Allen, Clapham and Dwyer, Harry Roy, Roy Fox, have been made stars just by broadcasting. Yet there is still a great body of music-hall artists who regard broadcasting as an enemy, a thing to be avoided, even fought against. Success on the air must inevitably mean stardom for the artist who achieves it. Surely that fact must be apparent. It is not only the artists who fail to appreciate the truth of that contention. We have made stars on the air, and then, when we have wanted them,

Another first! The first variety show to be presented by television. Sandy waves a sword and heralds in the single greatest revolution in entertainment. 1932.

we found that they had signed contracts, which prevented them from broad-casting.

It was a controversy that took a long time to resolve, but through all that time Sandy kept working both in music hall and on the air, finding that one helped the other, as was his original contention way back in 1928.

Friday 11th December 1936 was a day Sandy will never forget. *Sandy Powell's Road Show* in 'Situations', was scheduled for transmission that night. Around 7 p.m., just as they were finishing rehearsals, Bill Hanson the producer came into the studio. 'I've some bad news for you Sandy,' he said, 'your show is not going out tonight, it's been cancelled.'

Shocked, Sandy replied, 'It's a bit late to tell us, isn't it, Bill? Surely the show isn't that bad.'

'There's nothing wrong with the show,' replied Bill, 'but, I've just had word from the office that programmes are being rescheduled, and that somebody else is going on in your place.'

'Is it some other comic?' asked Sandy.

'Good heavens, no,' replied Bill, 'It's the King.'

'The King, what king?' queried a very puzzled Sandy.

'Our King, King Edward the Eighth. Your time is being used for his abdication speech.' The King's broadcast had been splashed around in the newspapers all that day, but Sandy had been so busy at rehearsals, he'd forgotten all about it, and never dreamt that his time would be utilised for this historic purpose. Sandy says 'I once had Will Fyffe deputize for me, but when I tell my grandchildren that I had a King 'dep' for me, they'll never believe it!'

The speech was relayed at the London Palladium not far from the studio, so Sandy hurriedly arranged to go there.

At the Palladium, George Black was in complete command of the situation. A great showman, and a person with a real sense of 'occasion,' he organised the arrangements in a masterly manner.

About ten minutes before the broadcast was due, the house-tabs were dropped, the lights put full-up, and the manager went out front and made the appropriate announcement.

Behind the curtains all the artists, stage hands and administrative staff were assembled quietly on the stage. The Crazy Gang, Flanagan and Allen, Nervo and Knox, Naughton and Gold, Monsewer Eddy Gray and Caryll and Mundy, formed a large group, centre stage. All were in dressing gowns. The other performers were in their stage attire, the stage hands in shirt-sleeves or overalls, the front-of-the-house staff – doormen, ushers, and box-office clerks – in evening dress or uniforms. They sat and stood around the stage and when the curtains rose, those on the flanks moved forward and sat on the run-out steps that led into the auditorium. It was a demon-stration of professionalism which could have looked theatrical if it hadn't been handled so skilfully and with such obvious sincerity. A few moments later, through the loud-speakers came the Speech of Abdication which was heard in sympathetic silence. At its conclusion, a roll on the drums introduced the National Anthem which brought the entire assembly to its feet and they sang their farewell to a popular King whose reign had lasted less than a year. Men and women wept openly and unashamedly. Sandy says it was one of the most moving moments he'd ever experienced, a time in history he will never forget.

Afterwards they went for a meal at the Criterion Restaurant in Piccadilly Circus, a popular eating and meeting place for theatrical folk. The place was buzzing with the sensational events of the day. Sandy's regular Italian waiter asked, 'Mr Sandy, aren't you on the wireless tonight?'

'We should have been,' replied Sandy, 'but our King abdicated and he went on in my place.'

'Oh you British,' commented the waiter, 'I'll never understand you people. In my country when things like this happen, we start shooting each other.'

'Whatever for?' queried Sandy.

The waiter replied, 'I don't know, but we do!'

Now in great demand for guest appearances on many different programmes, Sandy has memories of *Radiolympia*, a star-studded entertainment relayed from a huge theatre seating five thousand people, a building within a building, a complete theatre erected in ten days for stage performances which only lasted ten days. At the end of that time an army of workmen dismantled it in less than twenty-four hours.

Sandy also worked on commercial radio many times as one of the stars on the *Kraft Show*, sponsored by the famous cheese manufacturers, on Radio Luxembourg.

A less happy memory was his connection with an ill-fated show called *The Alhambra of the Air*, a pretentious programme which purported to blend art and music hall. Sandy, The Western Brothers and Robb Wilton performed before a studio audience of stuffed shirts from whom they could hardly get a titter. 'It was disastrous,' says Sandy, 'but you can't win all the time.'

John Sharman's Music Hall was a very successful radio show, a regular Saturday-night feature, which ran for a very long time because it provided consistently good light entertainment.

At one period, two comedians were used in the programme. One appeared early in the show, and the other near the finale for a comedy finish. For many weeks Sandy was one of the comics and the other was Max Wall. They shared a dressing-room, but, strangely, they never met. Both artists had other engagements, and the 'early man' had to rush away directly after he'd done his spot, and the 'late man' arrived at the studio just before he was due on, and neither saw each other until about thirty years later and then only by accident. Sandy was working at the Grand Theatre in Wolverhampton, and one night he was told casually that Max Wall was having a drink at a hotel, next door. This was an opportunity not to be missed so he went in to see Max who recognised him immediately. 'Do you realise Max,' said Sandy, 'that although we worked together in the *John Sharman*'s *Music Hall* thirty years ago, and shared the same dressing-room, this is our very first meeting.' It was quite a moment for both of them.

Sandy's own radio shows continued regularly right up to the outbreak of the Second World War. After the chaos that was caused in every field of entertainment, by the war, radio was slowly re-organised and decentralised, and broadcasts were made not only from London but also from temporary stations around the country. But with bombing becoming widespread, travelling around the country in heavily blacked-out trains that stopped and started many times because of pending or actual bombardment, the long journeys turned into hazardous – sometimes nightmarish – adventures.

Besides many *Workers' Playtime* shows in factory canteens, there were the regular programmes which were broadcast from Bristol in the West country, and Bangor and Llandudno in North Wales. The studios were usually in school rooms and sometimes in church halls; in Llandudno the Grand Theatre was used. Some of the programmes in which Sandy appeared were rather odd – as were some of their producers. A producer once wrote him:

Dear Mr Powell,
I am glad to know that you will be working on my show. I would suggest that you might do something in a humorous vein.

Sandy laughs every time he thinks of that one!

Rehearsing with his company one afternoon at Broadcasting House, Sandy was interrupted by Raymond Glendenning, the famous commentator, 'Sorry to interrupt Sandy, but we've got a spot of bother and I'd like you to help us out if possible, please.'

'What's up?' enquired Sandy.

'We're in the big studio next door broadcasting an hour of Ivor Novello's music and we've just had a message to say that there is a big raid on and it will be impossible for Ivor to get here in time for the show. Will you be a sport and help us out with a spot?'

Sandy replied, 'I'd be happy to help, but, won't it be a bit odd for a Yorkshire comic to go on in the middle of a programme of Ivor's beautiful music?' Raymond persisted, so Sandy did the spot. Since nobody wrote an indignant letter about it to *The Times* Sandy presumed his contribution couldn't have been too bad.

Sandy met Ivor Novello later and found him to be a great enthusiast for music hall and pantomime. Big West End productions were touring the provinces, because business was better there than in London where the air raids made it impossible for shows with a big cast to pay their way. Ivor was playing lead in one of his own shows in the theatre next door to where Sandy was working in pantomime, at the New Coventry Hippodrome. Practically every night when Ivor had a long wait he used to slip in to see the panto, standing in the wings completely absorbed in the action. He told Sandy that he loved the broad honest comedy and the wonderful rapport, the sympathy, that existed between the audience and the performers.

'I'd love to do a pantomime with you, Sandy,' he said.

'What part would you like to play,' enquired Sandy.

'I would like to be one of the robbers in *Babes in the Wood*; you can be the good robber and I will be the bad robber – I would love that' said Ivor. Sandy regrets he didn't sign him up on the spot. Sandy and Ivor Novello in pantomime together would have filled Wembley Stadium for years.

Television went off the air at the start of the war and the T.V. screens were dark for the duration. Instead of using the cathode tubes and techniques for transmitting entertainment, they were utilised in aircraft, at sea, under the sea and on land, giving out visual signals and squeaking bleep-bleeps to guide the planes and pin-point the enemy. Then with peace, eventually T.V. service was resumed with greatly improved equipment and more sophisticated techniques. Television programmes became more and more ambitious and were transmitted first from Alexandra Palace and then from Lime Grove. When commercial T.V. came along, the whole scene

Hughie Green – from radio to music-hall. The Empire, Shepherd's Bush, December 1934.

became an enormous power in entertainment.

As television came into its own again, Sandy made many appearances, it was a medium to which his talents were eminently suited. A list of T.V. shows in which he appeared would need many pages to record. He sometimes has a wry chuckle at the memory of the day in the 1930s when Bill Hanson, the BBC producer (who had previously been with the company that produced Sandy's records) suggested to Sandy: 'This new television thing wants someone to do a complete show, they've had people doing a minute or two, Sandy, what about it?' So Sandy did a forty five-minute revue, the very first on television.

One of his most vivid memories was the invitation to appear on *The David Frost Show* when it first came on to the screens. He was asked to telephone Frost and said, 'I understand that you want to speak to me Mr Frost.'

'You can cut out the Mr Frost stuff to start with. I'm only human like anyone else. I'd like you in my show.'

'To do what?' asked Sandy.

David replied, 'I haven't the slightest idea at this moment, but bring along some of your bits and pieces and we'll sort it out on the day. Rehearsal

Arthur Askey's first appearance in music-hall, after winning fame as a radio performer. The Empire, Shepherd's Bush, October 1938.

is at three o'clock at the Wembley Studios. See you then.'

Whenever Sandy was confronted with a 'We're not too sure what we want you to do' sort of situation, he had a bag packed with the props necessary for at least two acts. And so prepared, he reported at Wembley Studios in north-west London in good time for his three o'clock rehearsal call. He hung around the studio the whole afternoon, and didn't see David until about half-an hour before the show when he met him in the makeup room, where David was munching sandwiches.

'What am I supposed to be doing on the show?' asked Sandy.

David replied 'I've heard about your ventriloquist spot, I'd like that, and we'll also have a chat later on.'

'What about a pianist for my music?' Sandy asked.

'We don't use one on this show, I was given to understand that your wife plays the piano. Can't she do it?'

'But she assists me in the show,' protested Sandy.

David said, 'I'm on in a few minutes, you've got time, so please sort it out with the floor manager, he'll fix you up.'

So the piano was placed near the screen behind which Kay did her bits and pieces during the sketch and when their turn came, Kay, just out of camera, played Sandy's entrance music, then rushed round to hide behind the screen to do her part in the sketch, rushed back to the piano to sing the song – supposedly sung by the doll – and to play the exit music.

It must have looked very odd to the studio audience, but it evidently came over very well on the screen. Sandy thought that it would have looked even funnier if the whole episode had been screened. During the commercial break, he asked David about the conversation bit. 'I'll talk to you about Eastbourne,' and when he did, Sandy asked, 'How is it you know me, I'm an old performer, you're a young man and not really of a generation that knows much about music hall.'

'That's where you are wrong,' replied David. 'We lived in Eastbourne and I went to school there. Every week I used to go to the Pier and watch your show. I never missed a week, and that's how I know you.' That David, in his youth was one of Sandy's fans came as a great surprise.

David Frost invited Sandy to do another show with him at a later date. By this time David was commuting between London and New York every week. On the programme with Sandy was Hetty King, Randolph Sutton, the actor Peter Bull, and John Betjemann. This time Sandy was told in advance that David wanted him to do his burlesque conjuring act and a chat bit with Hetty and Randolph. So he wasn't too disturbed when, after arriving early (as usual) he didn't see David until he announced, 'My good friend Sandy Powell performing one of his classics, "The Master Magician".' But he was nearly put off his stroke when he saw that in the front row, the audience comprised a number of Teddy Bears of all shapes and sizes. They belonged to Peter Bull and John Betjemann who were avid collectors of Teddy Bears. Sandy says, 'They looked very nice, but they were a pretty dumb lot.'

Guesting in *Crowther's in Town* gave Sandy a lot of pleasure. The Palace Theatre, Cambridge Circus, in London was used. 'It was great to work in a real theatre, all plush, red and gold, on a real stage with footlights, and a packed house.' Sandy did his Ventriloquist Act about which the noted *Daily Mail* critic, Peter Black, wrote:

Sandy Powell's Dummy act is the funniest television I've seen. Viewers unlucky enough to have missed it should know that it is the old-pro-battling-on joke, based on the situation of a ventriloquist who can't really do it. Sandy has invented various variations. In one of them, in my opinion the funniest, the dummy becomes uncontrollable and disintegrates in his grasp. Sometimes its head is twisted back to front, sometimes it rises two feet from its shoulders, sometimes it detaches itself from the body completely, while the faces of the two continue to register the conscientious but baffled look of persons pushed to the limit but determined to brazen it out. It offers the most satisfying demonstration of pure fun-comedy I've seen on the box. In *Crowther's in Town*, he operated two dummies. One duly came undone. The other, a female of fiercely wooden aspect, stayed complete, but developed a wild, immovably fixed incongruous grin. The climax of the act had her purporting to sing 'Nellie Dean' while Sandy smoked a cigar and drank a glass of wine. It was really his wife behind the curtain. I would gratefully suggest that the joke would be funnier still if he let the audience discover this for itself instead of telling it. The audience passed into a happy tumult of laughter. Leslie Crowther's tribute was 'Wonderful act these old-timers had, I nearly wet myself watching.' Sandy's lovingly polished and worked-over act demonstrates the difference between it, and too many of the crude offerings offered through T.V.'s light entertainment.

During the years Sandy played a great number of different characters, immaculately acted to the last detail. This was clearly demonstrated when he hit the screen with *Suddenly It's Sandy Powell Again*. This was a programme in a series conceived and produced by Albert Stevenson. It proved to be one of the most successful series on BBC. Unfortunately there weren't too many good old pros about to make it a long series. However, Ted Ray, Arthur Askey and Cyril Fletcher were much enjoyed, and received great acclaim. One critic wrote: 'It provided the shortest half-hour I've seen on television for a long time.'

In this show Sandy had a fine old pro called Billy Whittaker, assisting. They played a couple of stout old ladies, one of whom confided, that 'she had been a Fan Dancer until she sat on her fan and broke it. It was an Electric Fan and I was very cut up at the time!' Sandy as a Chelsea Pensioner remembering the Boer War: 'They used to give us pills to stop us running after the women. I think they're just beginning to work.'

Through the years, Sandy has shone both in radio and television, and the demand for his services is still as great as ever – a wonderful thought for a lad of his age.

4

Seven Million Seventy-eights

DURING 1929 Sandy got one of the biggest breaks of his life. He went to see his agent Walter Bentley who was talking on the telephone when he entered the office and beckoning him to take a seat, Walter carried on his conversation. At its conclusion he said, 'Well, that's another good thing I've fixed, a recording session with Vocalion for one of my American acts.'

Jokingly Sandy said, 'That's marvellous, five minutes after these Americans get here you've fixed them up with a recording contract. What about us poor British artists, you don't bother about us.'

'But you don't sing,' said Bentley.

'I'm only kidding,' replied Sandy.

The next day Bentley phoned. 'You were bloody sarcastic yesterday about me only getting recording work for Americans; well I want you to know that I've fixed a session for a British artist – you. Tomorrow morning at ten you will be at the Vocalion Gramophone Company, City Road, London, for an appointment with Mr Bill Hanson their recording chief. We'll soon find out whether you're any bloody good!'

At that time Sandy was having considerable success with a sketch called 'The Lost Policeman', so when he met Mr Hanson he suggested that it might make a good record. 'All right, let's try it,' he replied. They got to work and it seemed to go very well indeed. A few days later Bill Hanson asked him to hear the recording and have a chat. Sandy thought that it was good, and Bill said, 'Our selection board like it, think it very funny and we'd like to put it out. I must be frank, talking records are not big sellers, except at Christmas, but we'll do our best.' Terms were discussed, and Bill explained that they proposed to issue it under their 'Broadcast' label, an eight-inch long-playing record with a playing duration equal to a ten-inch record. Price One shilling. 'You can have one payment of sixty pounds, with rights retained by Vocalion, you have no further interest in it, or, thirty pounds as the recording session fee, plus three farthings a side royalty.' Sandy decided to take the chance, and go for the thirty pounds, plus royalties. Little did he realise that the decision was to earn him many thousands of pounds, and would also be of immense importance in the way of personal publicity.

Almost immediately he went off to tour South Africa, his first visit there. a trip that took a long time because this was long before the days of air travel, and the excitement of the tour put the matter of his record right out of mind. By the time he got back home some months later he'd forgotten all about it. His first date was at the Alhambra, Leicester Square. There weren't too many dates in the book and he began to remind himself of what Walter Bentley had told him many years previously – that he might have been away from England too long, and that audiences would have forgotten him. But he went over as well as ever, and a further pleasant surprise awaited him.

Bill Hanson telephoned, 'Can I see you at the theatre tonight?'

'Sure,' replied Sandy, 'Happy to see you anytime,' and that was the first time he was reminded of the record. At the theatre that night, Bill gave him a few copies of the record and an envelope 'Here's the account for your first royalty fees, made up to date.' Sandy was amazed when he saw the amount written on the cheque – one hundred and seventy-five pounds. 'The next royalty cheque should be much better,' said Bill, 'because it will include the Christmas sales and that's the time when comedy records sell best.' He was right, for Sandy's next royalty cheque was in the region of four hundred and fifty pounds.

From then on, Sandy made a record every month, sometimes even more. He says, 'We churned them out like sausages.' Somebody must have liked them because 'The Lost Policeman' sold over half a million, and, over the years, sales of Sandy's records reached the incredible total of seven million copies, a remarkable number for those days of manual gramophones. Considering that it was long before the days of high-pressure sales, promotion schemes on T.V. and overseas sales, these figures are remarkable.

Issued under various labels like 'Rex', 'Broadcast', 'Imperial' and 'Victory', there was a total of ninety-seven records put on the market. They were very topical, always recognisable and the humour was simple, domestic and clean.

Starting with the 'Lost Policeman' as his first record, Sandy was later involved in being, respectively the 'Dirt Track Rider', 'Jockey', 'Mountaineer', 'Sailor', 'Fireman', 'Caretaker', 'Solicitor', 'Tram Conductor', 'Charabanc Driver', 'Doctor', 'Theatre-Queue Entertainer', 'Schoolmaster', 'Grocer', 'Taxi-Driver', 'Channel Swimmer', 'Polar Explorer', 'Magistrate', 'Footballer', 'Boxer', 'All-in-Wrestler', 'Zoo Keeper', 'Nudist', 'Film Star', 'Postman', 'Burglar', 'Dentist', 'Window Cleaner', 'Gangster', 'Airman', 'Soldier', 'Cricketer', 'Jockey', 'Broadcaster', 'Astrologer', 'Pools Winner', 'Detective', 'Housebuyer', 'Racehorse Owner', 'Blitzed Policeman' to name but a few! Sandy's records present a remarkable picture of the times as seen through the eyes of a comedian and his scriptwriters. This includes Sandy, because he wrote many of the scripts himself.

Royalties from his records alone earned him upwards of about twelve thousand pounds a year, which gave him an independence that enabled him to say 'No' to managements and agents when they offered too little money or dubious dates. 'Also', says Sandy, 'it gave me a chance to save a few bob for my old age.'

Many of Sandy's music-hall and radio sketches were recorded, and the publicity gained through these media helped business at the box-office. He was now billed as the 'Famous Radio and Recording Star'. The gramophone company printed advertising leaflets which were distributed at the theatres a week before Sandy's appearance giving a description of his show and including a list of his current records.

Other promotion stunts included autographing any of his records purchased at a particular emporium. This attracted large crowds, in fact in Derby the local newspapers reported that police stopped the traffic because of the huge crowd assembled in the High Street trying to get Sandy's autograph.

Christopher Stone, the distinguished doyen of gramophone critics, in his newspaper column which was headed 'Top Marks, Sandy,' wrote:

The infinitesimal shades of intonation and timing which makes the difference between a successful and barely adequate performance of this kind are also to be noted in the latest of a long series of best-selling records which Sandy Powell and his assistants have made. For reasons which are hard to analyse I think his 'Sandy Joins the Army' is one of the very best humorous sketches he has ever recorded . . .

A strange thing happened to the recording business when radio increased in popularity. The recording companies began to get very nervous, 'it was the beginning of the end' they thought, and panicked. They planned to cut down on staff and pull in their reins generally. One company told its employees that wages would have to be reduced, but, if they preferred, they could, in lieu, accept shares in the company. Many did, which later proved very much to their advantage.

The gramophone companies miscalculated very badly. What they didn't realise was that people hearing singers, comedians and orchestras on the air wanted to hear them again and again. A gramophone record enabled them to listen to their favourites any time without depending on the BBC's selection and timing.

Sandy was of course far too early to enjoy the spoils of the modern record boom, but he is very happy to have been on the scene in his days. He did it the hard way, but it was fun. One spoke or sang into a large microphone and if a mistake was made, one had to go back to the beginning and start all over again, even if they were the very last words or notes of the music. Today recording equipment is far more sophisticated, with tapes being used instead of the old shellac discs. They can be cut and adjusted quite easily, sounds and effects can be added and joined on as and where required: singers and instrumentalists can harmonise with themselves and quite extraordinary combinations can be achieved. Pop groups of four or five members can be made to sound like a large band, on record.

Gracie Fields was another popular artist recording on Vocalion records.

Sales of her records were also very large and someone at Vocalion had what he thought was a bright idea. Because Gracie's and Sandy's records each had a sale of half a million, if both were to record on a disc together, the sales would be fantastic. Their first disc was called 'Gracie's and Sandy's Party.' Besides the two stars, they had on the session Larry Adler, the brilliant harmonica virtuoso, Jay Wilbur's Band and Joe Peterson, a very popular singer on the music halls: Joe was a girl dressed as a choir boy, and very few people knew that the 'boy' was actually a girl. The record was issued in time for the Christmas season – just the record for a party. However, sales on this 'special' didn't amount to much more than the half-million usually attained by each artist. Tried on another occasion at the time of the Coronation in May 1937, a second disc was issued, featuring 'Gracie and Sandy at the Coronation', but the result was just the same. However, the foremost Catholic newspaper, the *Catholic Times* of London recommended purchase of the record, reporting that it 'describes the efforts of Gracie Fields and Sandy Powell to see the procession. This is amusing, and an added touch of comedy is provided by the fact that the popular pair travel to Piccadilly by *bus*.' The important magazine *The Sound Wave* enthused: 'Gracie and Sandy, Lancashire and Yorkshire in alliance to see the Coronation! Can you imagine the scrapes they get into? The arguments? The backchat? England's greatest comedy artistes at England's greatest event. It would be a shame to spoil your fun by disclosures, but it should be sufficient to say that we regard this as the funniest record issued for years.' Alas! It was all to no avail, sales reached just over half a million, and the combination was dropped.

Undaunted, the company came up with another brainwave; a sixpenny record that could be sold at Woolworths and similar stores. They selected two of Sandy's ten-inch record releases from the 'Imperial' label and re-issued them on the seven-inch 'Victory' label – exactly the same record, word for word. But strangely, even though it was cheaper in price, the idea

Sandy joins the nudists! And the people join Sandy.

failed. The public evidently preferred to pay more for exactly the same thing on a more expensive record.

As he became more and more involved in films, Sandy's record-making tapered off, and the only ones he made were songs featured in the films, such as 'Getting On Nicely Thank You' and 'Hear All, See All, Say N'owt', from Sandy's most successful film *I've Got a Horse*. These two songs became very popular with the public and the records were big sellers. Issued just before the Second World War were hit songs from his film *All at Sea* – 'Oh! Ain't It Grand to be in the Navy', by Jimmy Kennedy and Michael Carr, the famous song-writing team, and 'How Ashamed I Was' by his old pals, 'The Two Leslies'. Then, of course, the 'Lost Policeman' turned up again to recount his adventures in the Blitz, and finally in 1942 'Sandy Joins the Home Guard' which was the last record he made.

Those old 78's are now much-sought-after collectors' items. To complete the story, Decca issued a long player, 'The Best of Sandy Powell', and in 1972 the BBC had some short extracts in their 'Fifty Years of Radio Comedy' selection.

5

Moving with the Pictures

SUCCESS in radio, records and variety brought Sandy to the attention of the film-makers. The first to approach him was Pathe who were best known in this country for their *News Reel Gazette* which was shown each week in hundreds of cinemas. They also produced a special edition called *Pathe Pictorial* in which they featured famous artists from every branch of entertainment. They approached Sandy with a proposition for them to make his 'Lost Policeman' sketch into one of their fifteen-minutes *Pathe Pictorials*. At the time Sandy was working a few London theatres, so he could fit it in nicely. Most of the location work was done on the Downs near Brighton, and one of the most hilarious scenes featured the 'saucy kid', a part played by Sandy's own daughter Peggy, pleading for help from the phlegmatic Policeman (Sandy): 'Our 'erbert's fell in the river!' a line that had caught on with the public and was one of the most popular catch-phrases of the day. The part of 'our 'erbert' was played by Sandy's son Peter who didn't care much for the part since he didn't want to be a film star anyway.

Pathe Gazette newsreel often included a short item of entertainment, and Sandy was asked to do something from his record scripts, each of three to four minutes duration so he adapted a couple of them for filming. His daughter Peggy, then only six years old appeared in 'Sandy the Fireman' and Frank Lorden who was his feed in *Sandy's Road Show* did likewise in 'Sandy the Caretaker'.

During the filming of these shorts Sandy suggested to the Pathe director that he might give a chance to a young friend whom he described as a 'good young performer with a fine personality'. The recommendation was taken up, and resulted in the young man starting a career which eventually led to him being one of the biggest-ever money spinners in British film history. His name was George Formby Jnr.

George Pearson was one of the outstanding personalities in British silent cinema, and he got in touch with Sandy saying that he would like to do a full-length talking film with him. This was an important offer because George Pearson had established Betty Balfour as a film star in the role of 'Squibs' a lovable character who found instant favour with the public. This first film had led to a series of Squib films, all extremely popular be-

81

cause of their simplicity and sentimentality. The films were made to appeal to the ordinary man and woman in the street, who enjoyed stories from life with happy endings.

Pearson told Sandy that he and his partner Tommy Welsh had just returned from abroad where they had been taking the final shots of another big film. In London they went to see *The Jazz Singer* starring Al Jolson, whose first words spoken on film were 'Folks, you ain't seen nothin' yet!' It shook Pearson, and coming out of the cinema he said to his partner 'We're ruined, the film we've just seen has put us out of business.'

'What are you talking about?' enquired Welsh.

Pearson replied, 'Don't you realise what we have just seen has killed our silent film; it's as dead as a dodo. We've wasted our time and money, silent films are finished.'

Having the good sense not to waste time moaning about it, Pearson took immediate steps to jump on the band wagon of the new talking films, and this venture with Sandy was their first effort in 'talkies'.

The story was an adaptation of one of W. W. Jacob's tales, *The Third String* and was concerned with the hilarious adventures of three sailors. Sandy played the star role as 'Ginger', and the other two 'tars' were played by Mark Daly and Charles Paton. The film was made at the Stoll studio in Cricklewood, London, and was distributed as a Gaumont-Welsh-Pearson-Production.

With expert direction and the help of a talented and cooperative cast, Sandy's first film started him on the road to becoming a front-rank film comedian.

On the last day of filming when taking leave of the cast and staff, Sandy said 'thank you' to the call boy. He was a nice, quiet and very obliging boy and he said, 'Mr Powell, do you happen to know my father, he is in the music-hall business.'

'Really,' replied Sandy, 'what is his name?' The lad replied, 'George Black.' George Black, one of the most powerful men in show business, encouraged his sons to take an interest in every branch of entertainment and saw that they learnt the business from the bottom upwards. This paid off, for in later years they became successful in the profession and highly qualified because of their early training in films and theatre.

Producers Distributing Company next came on the scene with an offer to Sandy to make a film for New Ideal Pictures at their Triumph Studio, Hammersmith. Paul Thomson and Sandy did the script which included many items from Sandy's various music-hall acts. The film, called '*Can You Hear Me Mother?*' was directed by Leslie Pearce. Romantic interest was added by the charming and pretty young actress, Mary Lawson. There was a part in the film for a lady to act as Sandy's mother. This was given to Muriel Aked, a very fine character-actress. The story was about a Yorkshire mill-hand who performed comedy acts at local concerts, so when a London agent wired him an offer to work a trial week at a music hall in London, it created great excitement in the village. The boy was loaded with presents from the neighbours who cheered him off at the station. On the journey he fell in with a gang of card-sharps who were arrested before they could get back the money they had allowed him to win. On the train he also found an abandoned baby. With his winnings Sandy engaged a suite at a big hotel where he met a pretty girl. At the theatre his comedy act got the 'bird', but he got a second chance as assistant to a Chinese conjurer. Sandy married the 'girl' and when later, the baby was claimed by her real mother, his wife made up for his disappointment by telling him that they were having one of their own. Sandy telephoned his mother to tell her the good news,

'Sandy the Fireman', and featuring with him here is his daughter, Peggy, then aged six. A Pathé film.

and his first words were 'Can You Hear Me Mother' – hence the title of the film. It was simple, but obviously what audiences wanted. Preview showings all round the country brought enthusiastic response, and it was reported that P.D.C., the distributors, were snowed under with provincial demands for the film, which was not surprising, since Sandy's following in the provinces was enormous. The well-known film critic Frank Woolf wrote, 'Sandy's popularity in the variety, radio and gramophone spheres gives this comedy a decided box-office value and the reception from provincial audiences is a cert.' His summing-up was, 'General appeal: Very Good.' The trade paper *Kinematograph Weekly* reviewing the showing at the Adelphi Theatre in London reported. 'Sandy Powell, the radio, music-hall and gramophone favourite in a natural true-to-life comedy, is bound to appeal to every type of audience, old and young.' Another trade paper *Cinema* reported on the London trade show at the Adelphi Theatre:

Sandy with the scene-stealing Baby Ibbetson in the film version of Can you hear me, Mother?

Sandy's infectious urbanity and simple unaffected methods should prove immensely popular with the masses of patrons. The film is a shrewdly concocted blend of clean wholesome comedy with unforced sentiment, and is definitely a winner in its own class. Showmen catering for purely popular tastes may book it with confidence, and their box-office results should create a demand for more homely entertainment from the same stable.

Most of the newspapers mentioned the baby who stole many of the scenes. The important national newspaper the *Daily Sketch* called her the 'British Baby Picture Stealer'. She was a lovely ten month's old child named Ann Ibbetson, and this film collected for her not only plaudits but also a financial security for her future. Part of it came from a promotion which Cow & Gate arranged through a series of excellent tie-ups. They adopted the title of the film as a slogan for their famous patent milk product, and the nation-wide scheme provided for giant advertisements in which the film was mentioned in the whole of the national press. 'Can You Hear Me Mother?' was emblazoned on every advertisement. Sandy presented Baby Ann with a silver cup and saucer on which was engraved 'With happy memories of her first film'.

The *Daily Express* reported in September 1936 that the film costing about ten thousand pounds to make, had already grossed over forty thousand pounds and that it hadn't got half way round the country yet!

Tom Arnold next stepped in and contracted Sandy to make a film at the British Lion Studios in Beaconsfield, Bucks: a story of his own writing called *It's a Grand Old World*, and directed by Herbert Smith. The two ace British song writers Michael Carr and Jimmy Kennedy were commissioned to write the theme song 'It's a Grand Old World' which later became one of the most popular hits of the day. A strong cast was assembled to support Sandy, with pretty Gina Malo as his leading lady. Her singing and dancing was a big feature of the film and in some dance sequences she was partnered by Cyril Richard who had just come from Australia with the reputation as being their 'answer' to Fred Astaire. This, his first screen appearance in Britain, led him to a very successful stage and film career. The fine character-actors Garry Marsh and Frank Pettingell and a new child star, Iris Charles, made up a team which worked very happily together. This was another film that the whole family could enjoy, a story about a happy-go-lucky young man whose hobby was watching football matches and filling in football coupons. He fell in love with an actress at a theatre where he worked as props-man and later as a drummer in the village band. He won sixteen thousand pounds in a football pool and with the money proceeded to enter into a most bizarre and humorous adventure. He bought a huge mansion which was being used for shooting a film, and the funniest sequence of all was when he taught an escaped lion to roar. He believed the beast was an actor in a skin, and talked away calmly until the trainer came along to acclaim him a hero for capturing the lion. Sandy was fascinated by the way this scene with a real lion was handled by the director.

It was done by means of a 'split screen', a clever technique, that on the screen made it look as if Sandy was actually talking to a real lion. Again the film was a popular success. Oscar Deutsch, chairman and governing director of the cinema chain, Odeon Theatres Ltd., wrote to British Lion:

Having run *It's a Grand Old World* in North and South London and also quite a number of situations in the South of England, it is with great pleasure that I write to let you know the returns have been exceedingly good. As you know I was very doubtful whether Sandy Powell would be an attraction south of the Midlands area and I am surprised to find that the public thoroughly enjoyed this type of entertainment. I am now looking for some excellent results in the North.

British Lion Corporation now took over Tom Arnold's contract with Sandy, and his next film was announced as *It's a Fair Cop*, produced by Herbert Smith of British Lion Production in conjunction with Tom Arnold Ltd. A little later, the title was changed to *Leave It To Me*. Sandy was cast as a Special Constable and the romantic appeal was provided by Iris March, who had appeared in many C. B. Cochran West End shows. Franklin Dyall was a convincing Chinese villain and there was also a great team of character actors, Roy Jeffries, Davy Burnaby, Jack Hobbs, Wally Patch and Garry Marsh as a bullying police sergeant. The humour was of the robust music-hall type. The dialogue was somewhat innocuous, but Sandy's delivery ensured the laughs. Hilarious high-spots included some hectic action in which Sandy was the third member of an adagio dance team, posing as a woman, playing noughts and crosses on his chest and trying to pacify a couple of ferocious all-in-wrestlers. The contestants were Jack Pye and the Australian athlete George Penchiff, two of the most popular wrestlers of the day. In the film Jack was the villain, full of dirty tricks at which the audience howled and hooted in great anger. George Penchiff was the heroic victim of Dirty Pye. All-in-wrestling was (and still is) greatly entertaining – a mixture of highly professional skill and play-acting. Off-stage Jack Pye was a kindly and charming man. The story-line called for Sandy to break apart the wrestlers locked in apparent mortal combat because it had incited the audience to a near riot. Watching them at rehearsal Sandy said, 'You're not chucking me around like that.' Jack replied, 'Don't worry, if you follow my instructions you won't get hurt.' Reluctantly Sandy agreed and reminded Jack about his glasses. 'I'll remember,' said Jack, 'you won't get hurt, just relax and follow my instructions and you won't know you've been in a ring.' He was true to his word, picking up Sandy as if he was a feather-weight, whirling and spinning him around in terrifying style. But, apart from some giddiness, Sandy says, 'It wasn't too bad.' When they saw the 'rushes' the next day, he was astonished how real it all looked. Jack said 'I told you so, now what about taking up all-in, Sandy, you'd be a great draw.' Marco, the popular referee from Lane's Club in Baker Street, London, officiated in this film sequence. He was a master of the interplay between wrestlers, and highly expert in getting into a mix-up with them. His apparently innocent involvement in their violent action was the result of careful planning and regular rehearsal.

The film was a great success with the public, and there is no doubt that it established Sandy as one of the best British film comedians of the day.

Domestic comedy was featured in the next film, *Home from Home*, in which Kathleen Harrison played superbly the part of Sandy's wife. The script, written mainly by Sandy himself, was an adaptation of one of his most popular sketches called 'Brighter Dartmoor'. The story concerned the imprisonment of Sandy for a crime he hadn't committed and the consequent free pardon granted to him. *Home from Home* was full of comedy situations and domestic gags, the kind of film that used to be referred to by critics as 'typically British'. But once again, the box-office proved it did not have to resort to sex and violence for its popularity.

Whenever possible Sandy liked to play golf for relaxation, although he played very badly. To his great delight he found a man who was even worse than himself – his film director Herbert Smith. On one occasion Sandy

A concerned Sandy Powell gazes across to Mary Lawson in Can you hear me, Mother?

took him to a very exclusive, private golf course in North West London. Herbert played worse than ever, he spent most of the time in the rough or in bunkers, and it was a very triumphant Sandy who led the way back to the club-house. The club-house was full of members, and while they were drinking, one of them pulled Sandy aside and said, 'You've blotted your copybook as far as we are concerned, Sandy. Don't be offended, but your friend is Jewish, isn't he?'

Sandy replied, 'Yes, he is a very famous film director by the name of Herbert Smith, in fact he is directing the film I am making right now. He is a very fine person indeed.'

The man replied, 'Well, we do not allow Jews in the club and we do not like Jews playing on our course.'

His voice obviously carried to Herbert who came over and said, 'Don't worry old chap, I've hardly had a ball on your fairway, so I haven't played on your bloody course!'

Herbert Smith was British Lion's top man and he directed all the films

The Lion and I! The film is It's a Grand Old World.

that Sandy made for them. The next one, called *I've Got A Horse*, was the biggest money-spinner of them all.

Sandy had a very strong supporting cast with Norah Howard, Evelyn Roberts and Kathleen Harrison supplying the female interest and an excellent team of character actors, Felix Aylmer, Leo Franklyn (father of William Franklyn), Frank Atkinson, John Deverell, D. A. Clarke-Smith, Edward Chapman and Wilfred Hyde White, who played a very small part of a policeman in this film and who later became an international star of stage and screen. The songs 'Hear All, See All, Say Nowt' and 'Getting on Nicely Thank You', both written and published by Noel Gay, were very big sellers as sheet music and on record sung by Sandy. The words reflected the mood of the day:

> I'm getting on nicely, thank you,
> Everything's quite all right.
> Look at the lovely sunshine,

With Cyril Richard and Gina Marlo in It's a Grand Old World.

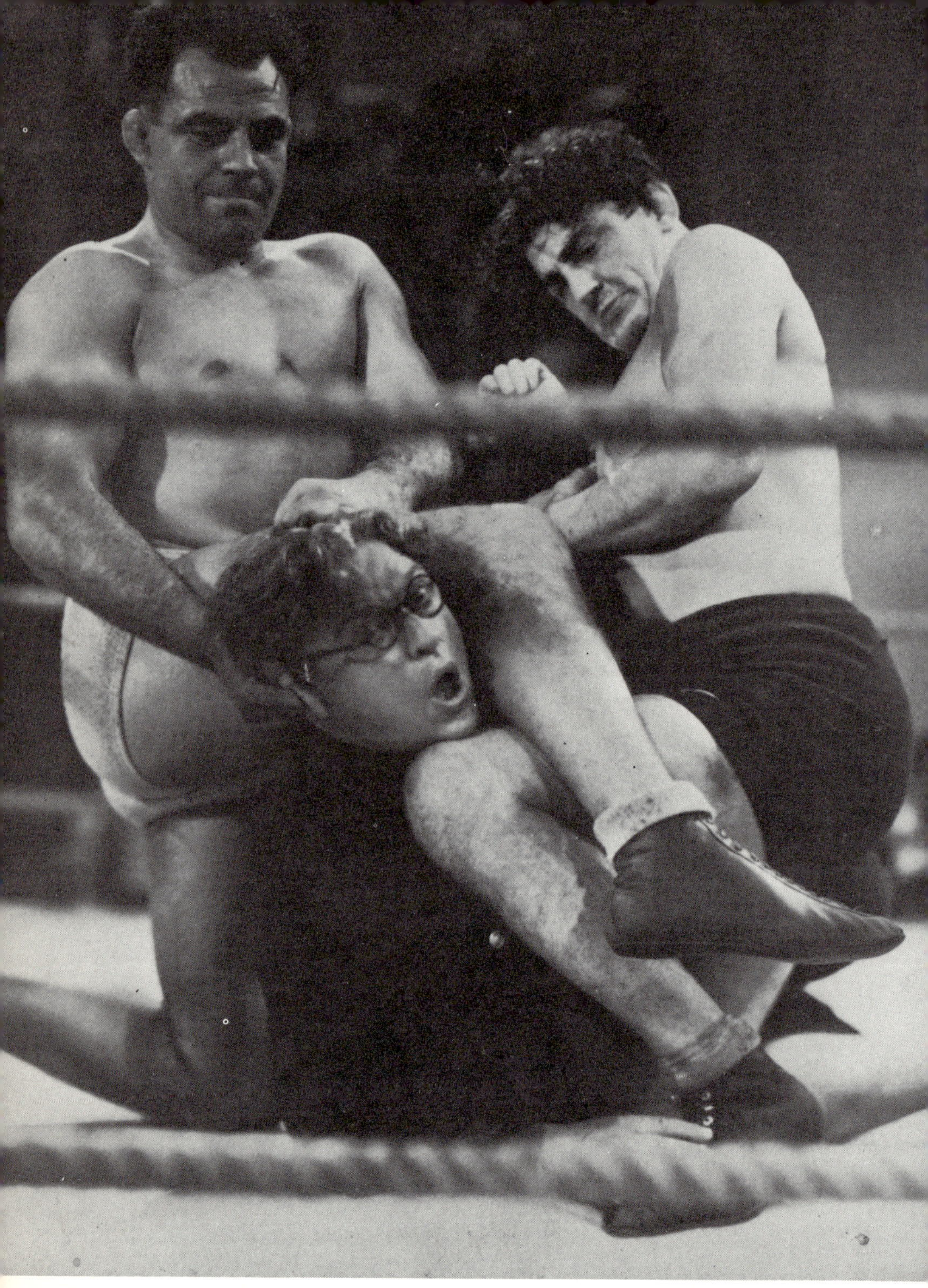

'Leave it to me!' said Sandy, and in the film of the same title Jack Pye and George Penchiff did just that.

Never a cloud in sight.
Everything seems so happy,
So really I can't complain,
Why even if it starts raining,
It's such a nice drop of rain.

It was typical of the flippant nonsense being sung at the time, showing unconcern with what was happening in the world politically. The film, however, established Sandy as a very competent film actor.

Just before the outbreak of the Second World War, Sandy completed the last film of his contract with British Lion, a contract that had made him the highest-paid British film comedian of the day. In *All at Sea*, Sandy played the part of one of the lads in Navy Blue and the strong supporting cast consisted of Kay Walsh, Garry Marsh, Gus MacNaughton, Franklin Dyall, Roger Livesey and Leslie Perrins. The film was advertised proudly as being 'produced with the full cooperation of the Royal Navy'. Theme songs had become an important side-product of film-making. Sales of the sheet music and a record sung by Sandy himself enjoyed great popularity. 'Oh! Ain't it Grand to be in the Navy' by Jimmy Kennedy and Michael Carr became

The dame and her bevy of beauties in Leave it to me.

very well known, and the chorus was whistled and sung with great enthusiasm:

> Oh ain't it grand to be in the Navy,
> One of the lads in Navy Blue.
> Oh for a life on the ocean wavy,
> 'Cos in the Navy you get the gravy.
> We love to do our duty
> For England, home and beauty,
> Especially beauty.
> Oh ain't it grand to be in the Navy,
> One of the lad's in Navy Blue

Published by the same firm as 'We're gonna hang out the washing on the Siegfried Line', it was patriotic stuff to suit the mood of the moment.

The Mancunian Film Corporation next engaged Sandy to do a film they advertised as Manchester's first Film Production, a Grand Musical Burlesque produced by John E. Blakeley titled *Cup-Tie Honeymoon*. The supporting cast included a vivacious young lady named Betty Jumel, Pat McGrath and Dan Young, a 'dude comedian', well known on the music halls. He was the originator of the 'Golfing Sketch'. Also featured was a fine character-actress Violet Farebrother, and Harold Walden who had been a famous professional footballer. *Cup-Tie Honeymoon* brings another memory to Sandy. A girl was wanted to play the part of his wife. They were having difficulty in filling this part, several actresses were suggested by the casting office but they had turned out to be either unsuitable or unavailable. A friend of Sandy's recommended a young lady who was working at a nearby repertory theatre, a Miss Pat Pilkington. She was auditioned for the part and proved extremely good. She later played an important role in the amazingly long-running television serial *Coronation Street*, her name – Pat Phoenix. There were no lavish sets and apart from the salaries of Sandy and his supporting artist's, it was a low-budget production which made a lot of money. Sandy's enormous popularity coupled with the public's interest in football, drew crowds to the cinemas all over the country. To quote the language of the times, it was a 'load of unrationed laughter, a sure-fire tonic in the war-time days of austerity, a sure cure for the blues', and that was just what the public wanted. As star of eight full-length films and many shorter features, Sandy made a significant contribution to British film comedy. Let us leave the last word to Herbert Smith who for many years was the production supervisor at the British Lion Studios, a man of high standing and reputation in the film world. Writing in *The Picturegoer Weekly* in August 1937 he stated:

I often wondered why this funny little Yorkshireman, still in his thirties, with red hair, spectacles and prominent teeth, is one of the biggest draws at the box-office in Britain today. He is a clever comedian, one of the most expert at 'timing' a joke that I have ever met or directed. But why does every man, woman and child in the Midlands and North and an ever-increasing public in the South flock to see him?

A letter shown to me recently from a wealthy man who owns three hotels in Blackpool supplied me with what, in my view, is the nearest solution. 'I must write and tell you', the letter read, 'after seeing you Mr Powell on the stage and in your film *It's a Grand Old World*, how pleased I am to be able to take my wife and family to see a show or film in which the leading comedian does not mistake dirt for humour.' Sandy is steeped in the tradition of British music hall and all it stands for. He was on the stage when most children are starting to learn their

Noel Gay's 'Getting on Nicely, thank you', from the score of I've got a horse.

alphabet, and from that day Sandy Powell has never cracked a dirty gag on stage, screen, radio or gramophone record. Brought up alongside the giants of the music hall, the best loved and most famous in the world, there has never been the slightest need to depart from his golden rule. Sandy feels that his audience is the family audience. He respects them. To date, I have directed Sandy Powell in two films. During the lengthy preparations of these pictures, I have travelled around the big towns in the provinces where Sandy Powell has been playing with his *Road Show*, he has been breaking box-office records everywhere. In Birmingham he made a personal appearance at a cinema on a Sunday night, at which I was present with a party of friends. So many people wanted to get in, that about thirty police were called in to control the crowds. The manager told me that about four thousand people were turned away that night. It reminded me of a première in New York or Hollywood rather than an ordinary Sunday-night film show in Birmingham.

Film work is a gruelling business, particularly in *Leave It To Me*, when Sandy had two days with two of the biggest and most powerful all-in-wrestlers in the business, it was hard going for him, but never once did he complain. He finished work on a Saturday and the following Monday was back again playing

I've got a horse, *with Frank Atkinson and Norah Howard.*

*Sandy questions a young and forlorn copper, otherwise Wilfred Hyde White
in* I've got a horse.

in his Road Show as usual. Most people would have taken a holiday, but not Sandy, he had fixed the date, and he would not disappoint his fans. As far as I am concerned, Sandy Powell is the best comedian I have ever directed, for two reasons. The first is that, unlike most other comedians with whom I have worked, he does not come into the studio and try to show us how it should be done. He is ready and eager to learn the technique of making films. Secondly, he is new material as far as films are concerned, and, therefore, I can mould him in the way I feel a comedian should appear and act on the screen. The most important thing is that everyone can go and see Sandy without the risk of being embarrassed. Which even today, is still a very important thing.

Smiling and saluting from the sheet-music of the song popularised in the film All at Sea.

This remarkable tribute from a top film-maker provides the background against which Sandy's films must be judged. Their enormous popularity was a reflection of what the public in those days most enjoyed, when the whole family went to the pictures together: 'Alas!' says Sandy, 'Those days seem to have gone forever – or have they?'

6

Variety Is the Spice of Life

ONCE Sandy had reached the age of twenty-one, he had become well established in the business and his date book was kept filled; but it was not all milk and honey. To be young and successful was uncommon in those days and some of the top stars resented the young artists getting laughs. Happily these were notable exceptions, and stars like Bransby Williams, George Mozart and Jimmy Jewel gave him help and encouragement. During his first Stoll tour Sandy often worked with Bransby Williams, a great actor who excelled in characters from Dickens, comedy and dramatic monologues.

When working around town on the London Theatres of Variety (L.T.V.) circuit he came into contact with George Mozart who was a top-liner with his thumbnail skits on real life. Jimmy Jewel (father of Jimmy Jewel of Jewel & Warris fame) was a top-star comedian when Sandy worked with him in the North. These men gave him infinite help and advice and were a source of inspiration. The habit of watching other acts had been firmly instilled in Sandy by his mother, and he realised that it provided him with a fortunate opportunity to learn from people who were masters of their craft.

Lily made sure that success didn't go to Sandy's head. When one of the acts on the bill boasted about what they had done or where they had lived, she told him to reply, 'My mother was born in the biggest house in Rotherham – the workhouse.' A fact she wasn't ashamed to admit.

Agents used to come backstage and tell Sandy what they could do for him. They were full of promises and good advice. A London agent, Harry Norris, told him that he ought to go abroad. 'Now's the time, son,' he advised. 'I can book you some good work in Australia, you'll do very well over there. It's a lovely trip on a luxury liner from Southampton, you'll have a beautiful cabin. The voyage will be a real holiday, you can laze in the sun with the blue sky above, a lovely smooth voyage and when you get there you'll feel as fit as a fiddle. The theatres there are magnificent and the audiences are the greatest in the world, you'll be an enormous success. Then when you return home, you'll be billed as "Sandy Powell direct from a triumphant tour of Australia". Everybody will be after you, you can't miss.'

He painted the picture in such glowing terms that he filled Sandy with enthusiasm and in this mood he went to see the man who was handling him at the time, Walter Bentley. When Sandy finished reciting the description of the proposed trip, Bentley said, 'That sounds fine, but do you know the real strength of going to work in Australia?'

'Yes,' replied Sandy, 'I go from Southampton on a big luxury liner . . .'

'Luxury liner my foot,' retorted Bentley. 'Listen to me, son. You have to share a cabin with three other men together with a horde of beetles and cockroaches. The ship will be turning somersaults most of the time and apart from being seasick you'll be bloody bored. With nothing to do except looking at the sea and sky for weeks, it'll drive you bloody balmy. When you

Sandy, twenty-one in 1921.

get to Australia you'll find that the theatres are dumps and the audiences a lot of bloody savages, they'll tear you to pieces and by the time you get back to England the bookers will have forgotten all about you, and you'll have to start looking for work all over again!'

Walter Bentley, who was Marie Lloyd's agent, was a 'character', prone to call a 'spade' a 'spade', but he was a shrewd and important agent with many famous stars on his books. He knew that what he told Sandy was greatly exaggerated, but he did not want another agent to step in and upset his own plans for this promising young performer. Actually, he was at that time in the process of booking him for some good work and had fixed his first date at the London Coliseum, one of the 'plum dates' in the business.

On the bill was a top American act called 'The Versatile Three', coloured artists whose polished close-harmony singing had caused a sensation. The next morning Sandy went to see Bentley who said, 'Sandy, I've had a good report about your show last night, Stoll's are very pleased with you. By the way, did you see my other act on the bill, "The Versatile Three"?'

'No, I didn't get a chance, but I'll make sure I see them tonight,' replied Sandy.

'You'll like them,' said Bentley, 'a great act and very nice fellows, straight as a die, they are three of the *whitest* men I know!'

Veterans of Variety. 1923

It was during this week that Lily officially retired from the stage and Sandy announced it at each performance. 'Here is Lily Le Main, my mother. Lily would then come on, take a bow and get a big round of applause.

In June 1921, one of the leading professional weeklies, *The Era*, featured Sandy on their front page, a large picture of him together with a report which read:

Sandy Powell, the popular Yorkshire comedian is a big hit at the Palace, Blackpool, with his new act 'Lost' which has proved a great success everywhere. During the last three years, Sandy has made big strides and is now in the front rank of comedians, and being booked by Moss, Stoll, L.T.V., MacNaghten and all the leading independent halls, right into 1929.

Long-term contracts came about because of the rivalry between the people who ran the big circuits and many of the stars were persuaded to sign ten-year contracts, some even fifteen-year ones. The wisdom of this was doubted in some quarters because, with guaranteed work so far ahead, a few acts didn't bother to change their material and went round year after year with the same old routines. The wise performers, of course, changed their material regularly, which was the reason for their continued success. Sandy became well known for his ever-changing material.

He was constantly having new experiences from which something could be learnt. For instance, when he finished a sixteen-week run in pantomime at the Theatre Royal, Leeds in April 1923, he was booked for variety the following week at the Hippodrome, a theatre that was right next door. On the face of it, it seemed crazy, yet it was a clever booking by those concerned.

The show was billed 'The Week of the Year – Old Stars and a New Star.' Sandy was the 'New Star' and the rest of the bill were stars from the days when music hall rose to its greatest heights, in the 1890s and the early 1900s: Arthur Roberts, Tom Costello, Jake Freidman, Charles Bignell, Leo Dryden, Charles Lee, Florrie Robina, Marguerite Corneille and Sable Fern. The idea was germinated in the mind of the London Palladium management to bring all these old stars together to sing their successes of former days. It was staged as *The Veterans of Variety* with Leo Dryden as chairman. He called the company to order and announced the name of the star who was next to appear, using a mallet which had originally belonged to George Helton, chairman at the old Barnard's Palace at Chatham. Mr Barnard was reported to have been the originator of the twice-nightly music hall, around 1870. It started because of the thousands of troops stationed in Chatham. Some had late permits and some had not, and Mr Barnard opened his hall at six o'clock to catch those who didn't have a late pass, and opened it again at nine for those who had. Leo Dryden, whose greatest sucess was 'The Miner's Dream of Home', was a great star who had many ups and downs, including a period when he actually sang in the streets to

Sandy with Arthur Roberts in 1923.

get a few pennies. Tom Costello, a great character player and singer, brought tears of laughter to the eyes of the audience with his rendering of 'At Trinity Church I Met My Doom', which he first sang in 1893, and another great favourite, 'Comrades'. Arthur Roberts, one of the finest comic singers of all time was, at the age of seventy, still able to 'stop the show' with his brilliant performance. Florrie Robina sang 'Not in England' which she first sang in 1896. Miss Corneille's 'Hello My Baby' sung in 1901, Sable Fern's 'What's the Use of Loving a Girl', 1902, and 'What Ho She Bumps' by Charles Bignell, first sung in 1893, were all in the show.

Twenty-three-year-old Sandy was frightened out of his life by the thought of having to work with these great artists, but he evidently rose to the occasion, for the *Yorkshire Evening Post* reported that 'Sandy Powell was the success of the week. A young star in the making, in the best tradition of music hall.' Sandy remembers that week as one of the greatest in his life. He never missed a single performance of these stars and delighted in the way they had of getting the audience to join in their songs with such gusto.

Sandy is the only pro still working today who actually worked with so many of the legendary stars of yesterday. He best remembers G. H. Chirgwin, 'The White-Eyed-Kaffir', a black-faced comedian who could vary his voice from a full baritone to a high falsetto and carried on an almost incessant back-chat with the audience. He played a one-string fiddle and sang show-stoppers like 'My Fiddle Is My Sweetheart', and 'Blind Boy'.

Others he recalls include Little Tich, a master of characterisation and a brilliant player of many parts. Off-stage he was a rather pompous little man who insisted on being addressed by his proper name, 'Mr Relph',

Fred Karno's Football Match Co. F.C. at Bournemouth in 1923. Sandy was 'Stiffy the Goalkeeper'.

and was very conscious of the fact that he had six fingers on each hand. Malcolm Scott, a supreme female impersonator was billed as 'The Woman Who Knows'; his artistry was perfection. So much has been written about Marie Lloyd that any words here might sound superfluous, but Sandy worked with her many times and can still remember her smile that was so simple yet said so much. She was considered the height of naughtiness, but she never delivered blue gags; it was the way the audience interpreted her words that gained her that reputation. Joe Elvin fascinated Sandy with his wild farcical absurdities; a great sketch-artist. Vesta Tilley, a wonderful male-impersonator who played many characters, including a man of the world. Nellie Wallace was a female droll who Sandy thinks was the greatest comedienne he ever worked with.

Grock the great French musical clown caused a sensation and was one of the highest-paid stars of the day. Stoll kept off other managements by contracting him for a period of fifteen years. Like many other artists, he became tangled up with the tax people, got badly in arrears, which he could or would not pay, and eventually left the country never to return. Many tried to imitate his act, but without the same success.

The list of artists with whom Sandy worked during the years would fill a volume. One of his regrets is that young performers of today don't get the chance to play the number of theatres that he did, nor to work with the artists of the calibre with whom he was able to work, and to serve the apprenticeship necessary to learn stage craft. He remembers playing the Royal Hippodrome, Liverpool, just before it was sold to become a cinema. Harry Tate was top of the bill, Robb Wilton bottom of the bill (which was equivalent to second-top) and Sandy and Tom D. Newall shared the

Max Miller, kneeling to the fore, in a concert Party in 1919.

'middle'; four comedians on the same bill, yet they did not clash because each was different in character and style. Robb was a fine actor as well as a music-hall comedian; his 'Mr Muddlecombe' and the immortal phrase 'The Day the War Broke Out' was a music-hall classic. In later years Robb and Sandy became the greatest of friends.

But, in Sandy's opinion the greatest of all the artists he worked with was Hetty King. A magnificent male impersonator, she had a meticulous care for detail. She had style, wonderful attack and a clarity of diction which enabled her words to be heard clearly in every part of the theatre, long before the days of the mechanical aids which artists use today to get the same effect. Hetty's songs like 'All the Nice Girls Love a Sailor' and so many others, will be sung as long as songs are sung. She continued to work, beautifully, right up to the time of her death at the age of eighty-nine.

Only twice during his lifetime was Sandy tempted to write to a newspaper. On both occasions his letters were addressed to that bastion of respectability and importance, *The Times*, and in them he forcibly expressed his regret that neither Hetty King nor Charlie Chaplin had been suitably honoured or officially recognised for their long service in the field of entertainment, and the pleasure they had given to millions through the years. Sandy's letters were never published. It is only in recent years that artists in the 'lower orders of entertainment' have been so honoured.

Reeves and Lamport representing Fred Karno booked Sandy to play the star role in a new Karno show at a salary of forty pounds a week. Fred Karno was a great producer of comedy music-hall sketches. They were top-of-the-bill acts of twenty minutes duration, and featured a big-name star. In this show his idea was to combine two of his most successful sketches, 'The Football Match' and 'The Smoking Concert', and expand them into a full-length show for twice-nightly performance. Sandy was the principal comedian and his leading lady was Jean Allistone, who later married the great wireless comedian, Tommy Handley. The show was a double thrill for Sandy because he was to play the part of Stiffy the Goalkeeper in the 'Football Match', a role that was previously played by his idol, Harry Weldon. Other greats who had previously worked in that sketch were Charlie Chaplin, his brother Sid Chaplin and Billy Poluski, so Sandy had something to follow.

The show opened at the Alexandra Theatre, Stoke Newington in North London where it did quite well. They also toured the provinces to run the show in before going into the Shepherds Bush Empire, then on to a complete tour of the Stoll theatres.

Unaccountably, the first house show at the 'Bush' was a diabolical flop; nothing went right. It was a very downhearted Sandy who returned to his dressing-room, the one that had a star painted on the door to show that it housed the top of the bill. Without a previous warning knock, the door burst open and there, reflected in the mirror of his dressing-room table, Sandy saw the figure of Fred Karno, just looking at him and not saying a word. After a silence, Karno said, 'And to think that I paid Charlie Chaplin three pounds ten shillings a week!' He then turned on his heel and left the room, slamming the door after him.

Fred Karno was an extraordinary man. He learnt the business the hard way, working the halls for many years before going into production and management. He became a master of the art of stage presentation and was a great showman. One of his great skills was the creation of a complete show from the slender material of a sketch. Some were entirely mimed; *The Fred Karno Speechless Comedians* was an enormously successful show, as were his other shows, the *Mumming Birds* and *The Bailiff*. The great comedian Fred Kitchen was one of his stars. Others not so well known at the time, like Charlie Chaplin and Stan Laurel, of Laurel and Hardy fame, developed in the Karno nursery and later became great stars. 'Karno' became a household name to describe anything that was outrageously funny or eccentric. British soldiers in the First World War called themselves 'Fred Karno's Army'.

Tom D. Gray's 'The Act Superb'. The presenters of tableau were amongst the most popular of the speciality turns in the music-hall.

Despite Karno's many successes, he had more than his share of disasters. His failures only occurred when he ventured out of the field in which he was experienced, and they eventually led him to bankruptcy and a sad death in 1941. The final blow came when he tried to create a large centre of entertainment on Taggs, an island in the middle of the River Thames at Hampton, Middlesex. Ironically it was Sandy who was called in by the BBC to do the commentary for a documentary on this Karno fiasco.

Sandy worked right through 1923 with the Karno Show. Despite its failure at Shepherds Bush, the subsequent tour was a big success. Publicity stunts of various kinds were used for the show. Practically every week, usually on a town's early closing day, a football match was staged between 'Fred Karno's Football Match Co., F.C.' and a local side like the police, St John's Ambulance Brigade, or similar organisations, and the proceeds were given to local charities. The event generated a lot of interest, raised sums for charity and was also publicity for the show.

Off-stage activities were great fun for the company. They were a happy crowd, except when Karno was around. He wasn't a very good morale-booster and more often than not was sarcastic and sometimes cruel. One Monday night, first house at Collins Music Hall, Islington Green, London – a theatre not renowned for its gentility – the audience was taking it out of one of the young second comics and giving him rough treatment. Coming off-stage after a tough spot, he stood in the wings awaiting the cue for his next entrance, his nerves were shot to pieces and he looked quite ill. Seeing Karno approach he said faintly, 'Mr Karno, I do feel funny.' Quick as a flash Karno snapped back, 'Then for goodness sake get out there, quick!'

At the end of the tour it was back to variety, and one night while working the Holborn Empire, Sandy was told they wanted him to go across to the Oxford to deputize for the top of the bill, Will Fyffe, who had been taken ill. It was quite a feather in Sandy's cap, and strangely, the compliment was returned some years later when Will Fyffe deputized for Sandy who had been taken ill in pantomime at the Palace, Manchester.

Another of Sandy's 'regrets' is the lack of variety in so many of today's shows. He remembers a bill on which he worked at the Alhambra, a beautiful theatre in Leicester Square in the heart of London's West End, in 1927. There were nine acts: Jack Hylton and his Band, Little Tich, The Houston Sisters (Renee and Billie), the brilliant American eccentric dancer, Ben Blue, Sandy Powell featuring a burlesque Russian dance and a hilarious sports medley, another young new comedian who was later to make the grade, Leslie Sarony, Daisy Wood (Marie Lloyd's sister), the comical 'Airman' Con Kenna assisted by his 'Pilot' in a fine speciality act and an excellent dancing troupe, The Rodney Hudson Girls. It was a real variety show and typical of what music-hall audiences saw in those days. Of course, the bigger the house, the more 'tops' they got, but the variety was just the same.

Sandy shared a dressing-room with Leslie Sarony, and from then on they worked together many times. Leslie, a small dapper figure of a man was dressed in full evening dress and sung his own compositions accompanying himself on the ukelele – an instrument and type of act that years later brought fame to George Formby Jnr. A talented composer, Leslie had over one hundred and sixty of his songs published, many of them sold a million copies like 'Aint It Grand to Be Blooming-well Dead', 'Changing of the Guard', and 'Rhymes'. He later teamed up with Leslie Holmes and their act, 'The Two Leslies', became a top of the bill attraction.

Sandy next enjoyed his first summer season at the Palace Theatre, in Douglas on the Isle of Man. It was a Julian Wylie spectacular called *The Douglas Follies*, and his success in that led him to being immediately booked for the next summer season in another lavish production by Julian Wylie. *Blackpool Follies* was presented at the Pavilion Theatre in the Winter Gardens, a huge entertainment complex, in that great resort. The cast included Naughton and Gold, who had been in the business since they were boys. They were inveterate practical jokers and stories of their comical wheezes will be told and retold by pros for evermore. Many years later they gained great fame as an important part of the famous 'Crazy Gang'. Sandy became involved with many of their comical capers because he shared a large double room with Charlie Naughton at the favourite hotel, The County, which was close to Blackpool's Central Station. Through it poured the countless thousands of holiday makers who made Blackpool the country's leading summer-entertainment centre. Alas, neither the station hotel nor the nearby music hall, Feldman's, exist today; they were demolished, presumably in the sacred name of progress.

George Black had taken over at the London Palladium and had revolutionised variety by a ruthless American-style speed and a strict timing of the acts that sunk the old easy-going stars. They were told to keep strictly to their allotted time, or else! By now, Sandy had become a popular name on the radio and prior to this Palladium appearance, Black requested that he mention the theatre in his broadcast. Sandy was given permission to do this and it was the first time that an announcement of this kind was ever made. Today it is standard practice.

The Palladium bill included the first appearance of a young comedian who was getting his first big break. His name was Max Miller and he and Sandy shared a dressing-room together. He was a sensation and in very few weeks became a top-line star. In Sandy's opinion Max was the finest stand-up comic of his time. 'The stage is the loneliest place in the world,' says Sandy, 'and you realise this when you are out there on your own. Many of the great stars like Harry Tate, Robb Wilton, Harry Weldon, Sid Field and others like them, were at their best as "sketch comics" working in combination with other performers – feeds, foils and stooges.'

Max Miller started in a First World War concert party, then in 1919 he joined 'Jack Shepherds Entertainers' working in Brighton, Sussex. He graduated into music hall and worked around in a very modest way for a long time before getting his big break. Sandy did well on the Palladium bill and subsequently worked all the General Theatre Corporation (G.T.C.)

Sandy Powell with Peter Kane, the champion boxer.

and Moss Empire dates. Then came a time when he had worked-in a new act, a Russian burlesque which he felt was right for the Holborn Empire. He asked his agent Mike Lyon to telephone G.T.C. about the date. When Mike got through he indicated to Sandy to listen on the extension earpiece so that he could hear what was said. 'It's Mike Lyon here, Sandy Powell's got a new act he thinks would be a winner for the Holborn, he hasn't worked there for quite a while – what about it?'

The reply was, 'Mike, you know we think the world of Sandy but he's been getting around a lot and we are giving him a rest for a time.' When he put his earpiece down, Sandy commented: 'That's fair enough, but I'm sure they don't realise how much the big sale of my records could pull them in at the box-office. I've an idea, Mike. Book me the two worst dates in the business. We'll get a show together and I'll put in my own bills on shares (of the takings at the box-office) I'll take a chance and see what happens.' So Mike contacted the Broadhead office and fixed Hippodrome Salford and Preston Hippodrome. At that time, business at these theatres was shocking, they were only taking around two to three hundred pounds a week. Sandy engaged two comedians, Billy Matchett and Peter White, formed a harmonica band, found a good singer, Paul Thompson, a line of girls and a speciality act called 'Tom D. Grey's Act Superb'. Calling the show *Sandy and His Pals*, and with himself billed as 'The Famous Record-ing and Broadcasting Star', they took six to seven hundred pounds a week at each of the theatres – trebling the business in fact. The MacNaghten office quickly got on to them to play their Palace of Varieties, Southampton, where business was also slack and Sandy agreed. He was anxious to prove his point. On the morning after opening there Mike telephoned Sandy. 'MacNaghten's have just told me that you did the best Monday night's business they've had for years. I'm coming down to Southampton today to see what it's all about.' Mike saw the first show, the house was nearly full, and bookings for the second house were heavy. He went backstage and Sandy asked, 'What did you think of it Mike?'

'Bloody awful,' was his jocular reply, 'But the audience obviously liked it. It must have been your mentions of that local fellow that did the trick.'

Sandy asked, 'What local fellow?'

' " 'Erbert, our 'Erbert" in that sketch and right through the show,' replied Mike.

'That's what I told you, they know him from my record and they've heard it on the air, in my "Lost Policeman" sketch. The record's sold half a million, it's a catch-phrase they laugh at. They've come in to see me in the flesh, which they can't do when I broadcast and record.' Mike Lyon was smart enough to realise that Sandy had tumbled to something that could be exploited, and from then on they worked on the idea of using Sandy's success on records and broadcasting to boost business at the box-office.

During 1932 they continued with the policy of a straightforward variety bill, and this developed the following year into the *Sandy Powell Road Show*, which was soon to break every box-office record in the country. It was a revue with plenty of comedy and good speciality acts; a show aimed to attract the family to the theatre.

Two backcloths were painted by a first-class scenic artist. One was a bright, colourful Tyrolean scene for the opening, and the other for the finale called 'A Night on the Embankment', pictured the River Thames, Houses of Parliament and Big Ben.

The company was strengthened by the addition of two solid acts and the line of girls was replaced by a trio of pretty and talented ladies who were already travelling with the show in another capacity; for one was married to the musical director, another to the stage manager and the third was in charge of the show's wardrobe and props. It was a happy arrangement which added to the spirit of 'family' which Sandy wanted in his company.

G.T.C., Moss, Stoll's and the principal independent theatre circuits soon took up every available date in the book.

Sandy Powell's Road Show worked its first big date at the Stratford Empire, a large and important Moss Empire theatre in London. It usually featured lavish productions and variety bills that were headed by several star acts. When Sandy's show turned up with their two backdrops, the resident stage manager asked, 'Where's your scenery?' Pointing to the two cloths Sandy's stage manager replied, 'You're looking at it, two cloths; for the rest we'll use whatever you've got!' When the resident stage manager got over his shock they sorted things out satisfactorily, and that night he was amazed how well the show was received. Business increased through the week and the box-office returns were excellent. Val Parnell of Moss Empires suggested that Sandy's show could go into Finsbury Park Empire, but, he warned: 'Sandy you know the kind of bills we put on at the "Park". Our audiences there expect a lot of big names, so you must book at least one big name to strengthen the bill. I'll leave it to you.'

Sandy tried, but the available name acts talked in 'telephone numbers'; some wanted more than the rest of the cast put together, so he took a chance and booked a good act called 'The Carson Sisters'. The week before their appearance at the 'Park', the bill had nine acts headed by 'Henry Hall and His Orchestra', Flanagan and Allen, Teddy Brown and six other first-class acts. It was some bill to follow. On the Monday morning when the company rehearsed with the pit orchestra, the resident stage manager had obviously been tipped off by his colleague at Stratford, so that he knew in advance that Sandy's 'gigantic production' consisted of two cloths, and he had the rest ready.

The show opened to a good first house and Sandy heard that bookings for the second house and the rest of the week were also very good, it looked like being a most successful week. The show went over with a bang and the next morning Parnell telephoned. 'Sandy, you've got the cheek of the devil. I left it to you to book a star name, and you get a little sister act. They were good, but you took a real liberty. But, apart from that I must tell you that I was standing in the foyer with the manager after the first house, you know I like to hear what the patrons say when they come out of a show. The house

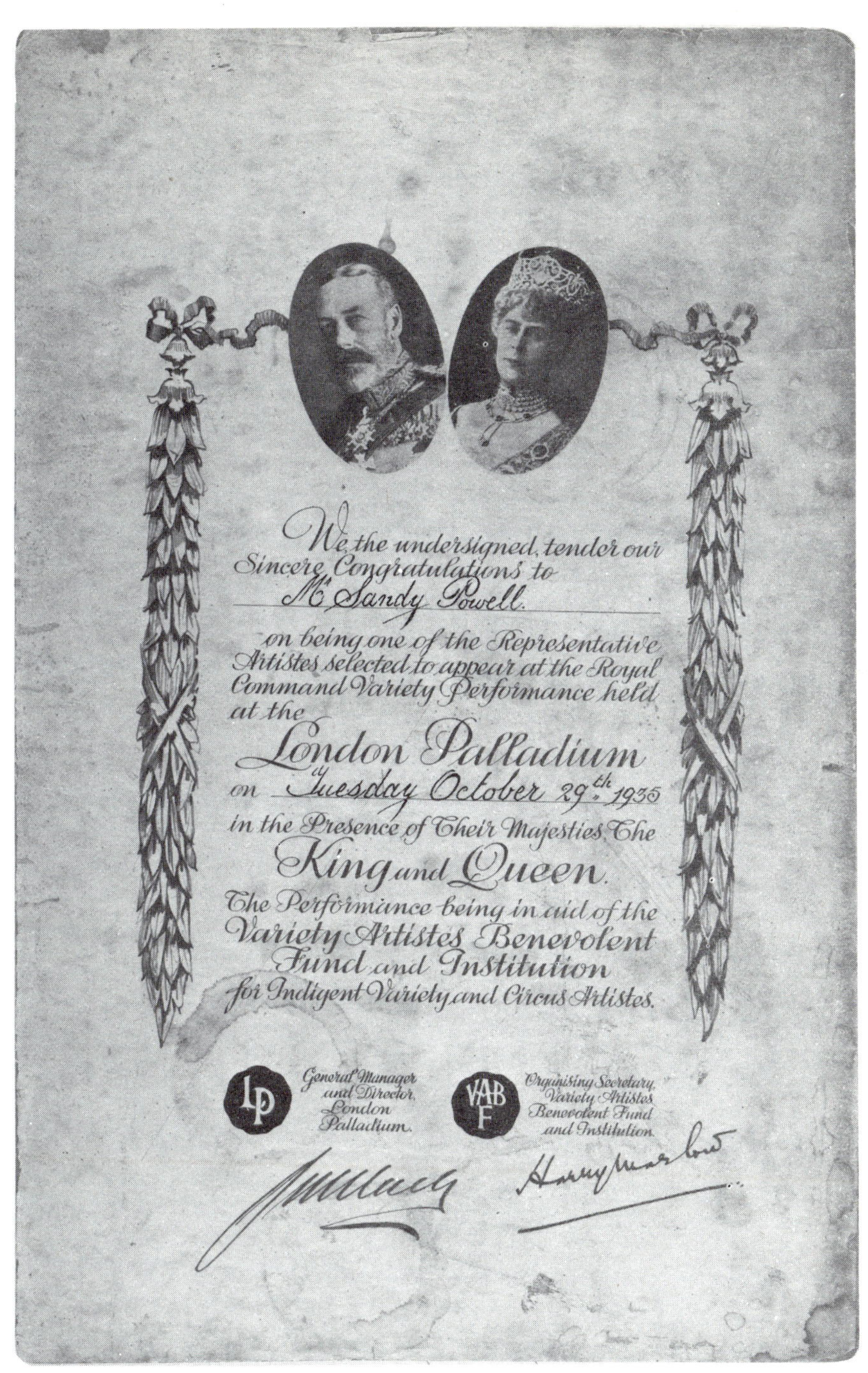

The certificate of congratulation given to Sandy by the Manager of the London Palladium and the Secretary of the Variety Artistes Benevolent Fund at the Royal Performance, 29 October 1935.

manager asked a couple how they enjoyed the show and do you know what the woman said? "I wish we could have more shows like this every week." And that, mind you, after the big bill we gave them last week!' Parnell really hated the idea of Sandy's 'tin-pot little show' as he called it, taking as much, and sometimes more, than the costly bills he booked for the Moss Empire and G.T.C. theatres during the years.

A summer season at Onchan Head, Douglas, Isle of Man, was Sandy's next venture. After his success there previously with the Julian Wylie spectacular, he was given a warm welcome, and his variety show *Sandy and His Pals* became very popular on the island. The company now included Roy Jeffries, and Syd and Max Harrison who had come to Sandy's notice through the recommendation of one of his second comics. They said, 'I know two lads working at the Windmill that I am sure you will like, try and see them.' So Sandy had made his way to the famous non-stop-revue theatre in London's West End. He saw the two men dancing and thought they were marvellous. Later, backstage, he offered the Douglas summer season to the lads who said that they were interested but, besides dancing, they wanted to patter as well. Sandy said, 'That's alright with me, what salary do you ask?' They wanted twelve pounds for the act (for the two of them), so Sandy booked them right away. Syd and Max Harrison were with Sandy for quite a few years during which time they became polished performers and went on to become headliners in their own right. The brothers married while working with Sandy, and each had a son, who later made the grade in the business as Hope and Keen, now well-known on television and in cabaret, and have also appeared in a Royal Show. Watching them work you can see the style of their fathers' acts. Roy Jeffries also stayed with Sandy for many years and became one of the finest 'feeds' in the business, appearing with Sandy in the Royal Performance as well as his films.

Sandy and His Pals worked four seasons at Onchan Head and became established favourites with both British and Irish holiday visitors to the Isle of Man.

Moss Empires arranged with Sandy that when he finished in Douglas, he would make his way across the Irish Sea to work the following week at the Liverpool Empire with his *Sandy Powell Road Show*.

A few weeks before they were due to open in Liverpool, Black wrote to Sandy, stressing the importance of him booking a big-name star to strengthen the show. The Empire was a large capacity house and the biggest and most lavish of the touring shows had to include one or two stars in addition to those already in their show. Sandy found that, as before, stars who were available wanted an enormous salary; then he had a brainwave. He knew and admired a young boxer who was making a name for himself, Peter Kane. He was known as 'The Golborne Hurricane', and was idolized in Liverpool. He got in touch with Ted Denver, Kane's manager, and intimated that he'd like the lad in his show at the Empire, doing some skipping, ball-punching, shadow-boxing and finishing off with a three-rounds bout with a sparring partner. Peter Kane liked the idea and all was

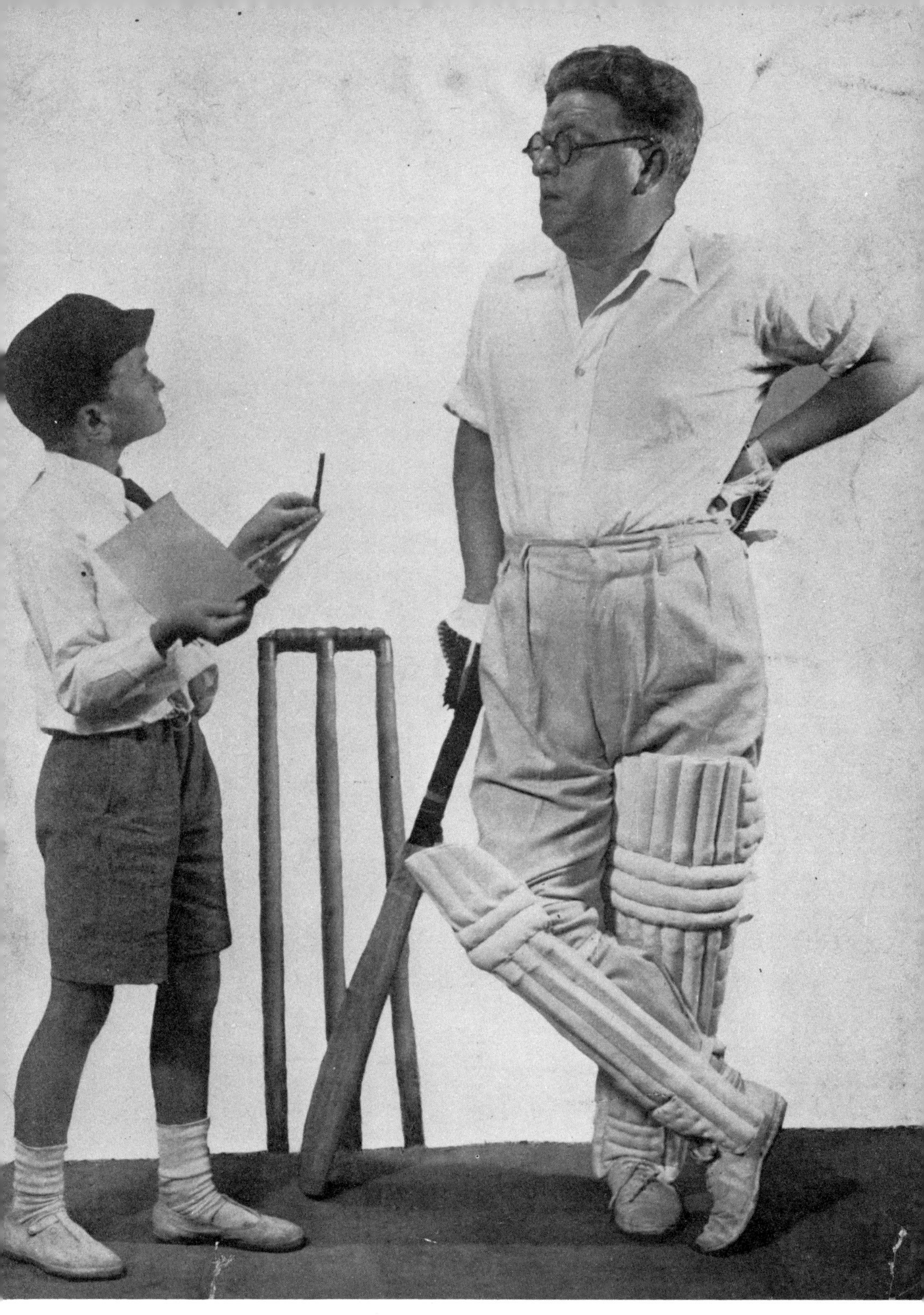

'*The Test Match*' – *Sandy's contribution to the Royal performance in 1935.*

set. The moment the word went out that he would be appearing with Sandy, it started a rush to the box-office and before the show even started, the house was sold out for the entire week. The show itself was an emphatic success, and the week after, George Black sent Sandy his congratulations for finding such a marvellous added attraction. 'I know that it must have cost you a lot of money,' he wrote, 'so please accept the enclosed cheque as a small token of my appreciation.' It was a cheque for fifty pounds, which Sandy thought was a nice gesture.

Like Val Parnell, it was a mystery to George Black how Sandy could fill theatres with what Black described as 'Sandy's sixpenny-worth of a show. This was brought out when Sandy played the Empire, Newcastle-on-Tyne. When they got there they found that advanced bookings for the show were almost up to capacity. Just before the first house, Dicky Reed the Northern-area superviser said that George Black had arrived. 'I'm glad we've got a good house for him,' said Sandy, and he told the company that 'G.B.' would be out front, 'So, let's give him an extra good show.' They all set out to do a little more than their best and put on a superb performance. After the first house 'G.B.' went to see Sandy. 'I hope you enjoyed the show Mr Black,' he said.

A trio of artistes taking time off from Jack Taylor's King Revel *at the Hippodrome, Blackpool in 1938. To Sandy's left are Norman 'Over the Garden Wall' Evans and Nat Gonella, one of our finest native jazz trumpeters.*

'I didn't see it,' replied Black.

Puzzled, Sandy asked, 'Are you leaving it for the second house?'

G.B. said 'No, I won't see that either, and if you think that sounds strange, I'll explain. The shows I put on cost me thousands. Top stars, lavish scenery and dresses, expensive producers, trap doors, revolving stages, trick lighting and all that; it costs me a fortune. I come up here and find that your sixpenny-worth of a show with two back cloths packs them in and you play to capacity business. If I was to watch your show from the front I'd come backstage afterwards and tell you that you ought to have a steam engine racing across the stage, spectacular scenes, loads of show girls, expensive dresses and scenery and three of four big names to back you up. I'm better off minding my own business and being content seeing your box-office returns that make money for both of us.'

That week at Newcastle gave Sandy another happy memory when he was visited backstage by the great Scottish comedian Harry Lauder. He told him how much he had enjoyed the show: 'I'll be in tomorrow night to see you again, laddie, and I hope to have a little something for you.' He kept his promise and the next night he presented Sandy with two lovely trout. 'I'm up here on a little fishing holiday, Sandy, and I caught these especially

Duggy Wakefield and Sandy at the links in Blackpool, 1938.

for you!' Sandy wished that he had had them stuffed, it would have been a unique reminder of the meeting with one of the all-time greats.

More and more American acts were coming to work in Britain, and Sandy found them to be very 'professional' in their attitude, apart from the slickness and polish they put into their act. This was brought home to him forcibly when he was asked to participate in a presentation at the Holborn Empire. The first half was taken up with five big American acts: Joe Jackson, the fabulous comedy act 'Stealing a Bicycle', Vic Oliver, the talking and fiddling comedian whose sensational success decided him to live in England (he later married Sarah Churchill, daughter of the late Sir Winston Churchill), the beautiful Gypsy Nina, Gene Sheldon, Ace Banjoist, and a coloured dancer, probably the finest-ever tap dancer, Bill Robinson, who originated the 'Staircase Dance'. He was an old man then but danced with youthful agility. He taught Hollywood and Vaudeville stars how to dance. The second half was Sandy's show, and Val Parnell's idea was that in his closing scene on the Embankment, he would bring on the American acts, introducing them one by one, to make a spectacular finale. Sandy was dubious that the American stars would hang around until the end of the show just to be introduced again. 'You'll find them very cooperative,' said Parnell, and he was right. Every one came on in their stage dress and properly made up, even Joe Jackson whose makeup was very intricate and took a long time to put on.

It was now coming up to Sandy's 'peak year,' the one he describes as his 'mad year', when every move he made in the business came up trumps. The name 'Sandy Powell' on a bill meant full houses. But his crowning joy came when he received a letter from The Variety Artistes Benevolent Fund which informed him that he was invited to appear in the 1935 Royal Performance. He was booked to work at the Sunderland Empire the week of the show, but Moss Empires were pleased to cooperate. Sandy opened as usual, on the Monday night, then made an overnight dash to London after the show, had a short nap in his London flat, and then went off on Tuesday morning to the London Palladium for the gruelling rehearsals. He had made sure his mother had a seat; for her also it was an important occasion. Thirty years ago he had worked on the stage for the first time, helping with her marionette act, touring round the dumps and here he was at one of the world's greatest theatres to perform before their Majesties, King George and Queen Mary.

The royal bill glittered with stars of the first magnitude. From America came the Diamond Brothers, brilliant performers with a fantastic running-gag in which a large wooden board from side-stage, crashed down, narrowly missing one of the brothers. This was repeated several times, and each time it seemed as if it couldn't possibly miss. Others in the line-up included Joe Jackson with his crazy bicycle act, Anton Dolin and Jessie Matthews, The Western Brothers, Boy Foy, the seventeen-year-old Juggler performing incredible feats while mounted all the time on a unicycle, Stanley Holloway in a deliciously phrased Lancashire monologue, the sensational roller skating of the Three Cossacks and the favourite radio duetists, Elsie Carlisle and Sam Browne. Sandy's skit about the Test Match obviously captured the fancy of the Royal Party, who much enjoyed the joke that he found himself in the Test Team because of a mistake – he had really applied for the Means Test. It was a delightful cricket satire with Sandy as the batsman, Roy Jeffries as the team captain and Jimmy Fletcher as a saucy kid. The show was stolen by an American act, Will Mahoney, who, with his xylophone playing and dancing, was the undoubted hit of the show. In addition to these featured acts, the show also included two scenes from the London Palladium production, *Round About Regent Street*, starring Flanagan and Allen, Nervo and Knox, Naughton and Gold, and a number of other artists.

Jimmy Fletcher who worked with Sandy in the 'Test Match' sketch, was one of many young hopefuls that he discovered while on tour. Jimmy was the youngest performer to appear in a Royal Performance. Wherever he worked, Sandy held auditions for young people; he found Jimmy in Sheffield when, one morning at the Empire, he sang 'Schubert's Serenade' and everybody in the theatre stopped working. The cleaners put down their mops and pails, the stage hands stopped whatever they were doing and listened to this silver-voiced youngster. Sandy knew immediately that he was on to a winner and booked him immediately to start the very next week at the Empire, Leeds. Sandy billed and dressed him as 'The Singing Newsboy', and he stopped the show at every performance.

The auditions were not advertised but word got round and if, any morning, youngsters came to the theatre, Sandy gave them a hearing. If he thought they had a chance to succeed he did all he could to get them on, sometimes putting them into his radio or stage shows. He believed in getting them on stage as quickly as possible because, as he said with Yorkshire directness, 'It's the best way. Throw them in at the deep end. If they've got it, they'll make it.' Other discoveries, apart from Jimmy, included Jenny McAndrew, a brilliant schoolgirl ventriloquist, and Patricia Rich, daughter of Albert Rich of Rich and Galvin, the simultaneous dancers. Pat had a lovely voice and did well on Sandy's radio show. Margaret Stott, who was working in a mill at Haslingden in Lancashire, was another successful young singer. Sandy dressed her in a stage version of her working clothes, including shawl and clogs, and billed her as 'The Mill Girl Soprano'.

Touches like these made Sandy's show successful everywhere they worked. It was remarkable how his style and comedy was accepted so readily in every part of the country. It was notorious in the profession, that an artist or a show could be a success in some towns, but would 'die a death' in others. There have been many fanciful theories about this, but to Sandy the answer has always been simple; good variety, plenty of fun, and keep it clean. In Scotland, the *Edinburgh Dispatch* reported:

There is no more likeable comedian on the stage than Sandy Powell. His genial manner, cheerful smile and homely type of humour, have not only made him a tremendous favourite in the music halls, but have established him as a popular broadcaster and as one of the greatest mirth-makers of the moment. *Sandy Powell's Album* at the Empire features 'The Ginger Beer Guards' a boisterous burlesque of Drills and Dolls. The Harmonica Band producing real music. Presto and Campo, acrobats of seemingly effortless skill and great humour, The Billy Shenton Trio dance with grace and charm and Gloria Santa Fe in an admirable solo acrobatic turn. The Mechanical Robot is a novel and baffling mystery, answering questions by members of the audience, and Jimmy Fletcher the silver-voiced Newsboy Singer. Sandy's contributions include 'The Broadcasting Studio', 'The Stage Door' and he is a consummate purveyor of comedy. He does things in an original way – as a Test Cricketer, A Guardsman, a Boxer who has had an unfortunate experience, and as a coffee-stall-keeper. He also croons and conducts a Harmonica Band. It's all good fun and noise, with something to suit everybodys taste.

From Ireland, there was a report about his show at the Belfast Opera House:

The line-up for the finale at the Royal Performance in 1938.

Sandy Powell marked himself out as one of those rare beings, a genuine comedian. Even to those quite unfamiliar with his name or work, although broadcasting has made for him here many friends before his personal appearance, he at once established his claim to recognition. His manner, his walk, and his features evoked that spontaneous pleasure which only the artist can arouse. But it was not only his manner or even humour that shone out clearly, that proved him the comedian, but a quaint indescribable pathos that belongs only to the genuine comic.

From Wales, a report from the New Theatre, Cardiff:

Raise your hats to Sandy Powell with his *Road Show*, for they give you entertainment that is intensely amusing, varied and yet not the slightest suggestion of even a risque joke. This mild-mannered little man with the Carroty hair and North Country accent is something the stage has been needing for a long time. someone who can prove that a clean show is funnier than a smutty one. If proof were needed, last night's audience provided it. They lapped up the bill and demanded more. I can tell you now with all the sincerity at my command that Sandy Powell and His Road Show is one of the shows in town you cannot miss.

In the Midlands, the *Birmingham Weekly Post*:

Comedians crack smoking-room gags without troubling to give them a drawing-room twist, and freedom in every direction is the order. We are told that this is what the public wants, that the age of mealy-mouths is over, and so on. Often enough one is tempted to believe such statements, until a comedian like Sandy Powell, who has never said a 'blue line' in his life, comes along and breaks box-office records. So what does the public want?

From the great shipping port in the north-west, the *Liverpool Post:*

Sandy Powell's Road Show at the Shakespeare does not rely on spectacular scenes and effects for his success but on a perfectly balanced programme of talented artists, each an adept in his or her own particular field. The fun – most of it being provided by Sandy himself, is homely and wholesome, and the farcical sketches are excellent. Syd and Max Harrison are clever exponents of acrobatic and eccentric dancing. Clara Kenyon, the Violinist, and Jimmy Fletcher, the singing newsboy provide pleasing musical items, Betty Jackson's Dog and Monkeys add interest to the programme, particularly for the youngsters, and the Ten Moonbeams present a quick-fire act which embodies first-class dancing. Sandy also introduced a newcomer, a songstress formerly a mill girl, another of his discoveries, Marjorie Stott.

One of London's leading theatrical papers, *The Era*, reported:

In a neat little speech at the close of the first show at Stratford Empire, Sandy Powell expressed his opinion that the magnificent reception accorded to him and his company was a tribute to his efforts in providing good, clean entertainment. It is no exaggeration to say that it would be impossible to find a single feature of his *Road Show* which could possibly cause offense to anyone. The large queue which waited patiently for admission to both houses paid an effective tribute to Sandy's immense popularity. While there was not one dull moment, perhaps the most enjoyable scene was the 'Broadcasting Studio', the pièce de resistance of which was the burlesque of Al Jolson singing 'Sonny Boy'. Jimmy Fletcher, Sandy's 'find', charmed everyone with his singing. Sandy has been described as 'the lovable comedian' and this description fits him perfectly. 'The Test Match', much enjoyed by the audience, is the sketch which made the King and Queen laugh at the recent Royal Performance at the Palladium. This attraction has been breaking records throughout the country and Sandy himself is undoubtedly responsible for this.

From these few random reports one can get a picture of what Sandy represented to music hall. He was undoubtedly a major force in popular entertainment.

Jack Taylor was a man who put on spectacular shows for the Blackpool Tower Company at the huge Opera House. He had a quarrel with them and decided to go into opposition at the Hippodrome Theatre just along the road. He engaged Robert Nesbitt (who produces the Royal Performance) and a cast headed by Sandy. Appearing were Nat Gonella and his Georgians, comedian Norman Evans, whose 'Over the Garden Wall' was a classic of domestic humour, the hilarious Duggy Wakefield and His Gang, the sensational adagio dancers Katrina, Vadio and Hertz, an American dancing star Gloria Gilbert, a line of beautiful dancers and a big supporting cast. At one of the rehearsals Sandy was sitting with Jack Taylor when he asked to see the 'Seven Seas Scene'. Sandy remarked, 'What a lovely set, and those dresses look marvellous.'

Taylor replied, 'Yes, but it's bloody expensive, when you have Nesbitt it costs money. With him everything has got to be just right; his bloody tar has cost me thousands.'

'How can tar cost you thousands?' asked a puzzled Sandy. To this Taylor replied: 'Every time I say to Nesbitt "Bob that doesn't look too bad, it'll do," he says, "Now Jack, don't let's spoil the ship for a ha'porth of tar!" ' Jack Taylor was forthright in speech and attitude, but he did put on some very lavish spectaculars and this show called *King Revel* was a great success. It didn't shatter the Tower Company as Jack had hoped (they were too big a force in Blackpool), but he did very well out of it financially.

Sandy was again asked to appear in another Royal Performance which took place in November 1938 at the London Coliseum. But this time it was in a different capacity to the 1935 show, when he was one of the featured artists.

He appeared as one of the supernumeraries in a 'Lambeth Walk' scene from *Me and My Girl* which was currently playing the Victoria Palace, with the show's principal's Lupino Lane, George Graves and Teddy St. Dennis leading two hundred and fifty artists dancing the Lambeth Walk. Almost everybody in the business was in this scene, it was a brilliant, glittering and fantastic spectacle. The super finale to a Royal Show had started in the early thirties; not only did it provide a flamboyant scene, but it also gave a great

number of artist's a chance to appear in the show. Some shrewd managements used to bill acts as 'Direct from the Royal Performance', when all
they had done was to have walked on or stood around in the finale. This
show was the last Royal Performance for seven years because war came
and they were not restarted until November 1945.

Sandy was next inveigled into musical comedy by Charles Henry. He
was the man who, as touring manager of a revue, had sacked Sandy on the
very first night of the show in Eastbourne, nearly twenty-five years previously. Now he was a famous producer and had approached Sandy to take
the principal comedian's role in the number-one touring company of the
big London success, *Hold Everything*. The part was that of a boxer and had
been played in the London production by George Gee.

'This isn't my stuff, Charlie,' protested Sandy. 'Me in a musical? I won't
fit in.'

'Of course you will,' said Charles Henry, 'You had a sketch on the halls
about a boxer and one of your best records was "Sandy the Boxer". Besides,
it will make a nice change from working the halls. These musical comedy
people are nice, gentle people, you will enjoy working with them.'

Sandy finally agreed and eventually the show opened at the Finsbury
Park Empire. The tour that had been fixed was in the number-one provincial theatres. The big number of the show was 'You're The Cream In
My Coffee', sung and danced by Sandy and the leading lady. During the
routine the girl kicked up her leg to land on Sandy's shoulder, while he
turned his head simultaneously towards the opposite shoulder. This was
followed by her leg-kick to the other shoulder, but, on the opening night it
was mistimed, and Sandy was kicked heavily on his jaw. It loosened two
front teeth, which later caused him to have all his teeth removed. But more
was to follow that night. In a later scene an actress had to slap Sandy's face.
Presumably because of first night nerves, she gave him a real clout. At that
moment Sandy thought his ear-drum was broken. After the show he
showed his bruises to Charles Henry. 'I ought to demand danger money,'
he told him. 'I thought you said they were nice people, the only time I
didn't get hurt was in the actual boxing scene!'

Another summer season and then on the road touring in variety kept
Sandy busy during the uncertain year that led up to the outbreak of the
Second World War.

7

Wartime Entertainment

T HE Second World War started in September 1939. German bombers were expected any moment and all theatres were ordered to close immediately. *The Sandy Powell Road Show* was, in consequence, closed, and all the artists returned to their homes, but were asked to stand by for further news when the situation clarified. The expected 'blitz' did not happen and a few weeks later Sandy received a telegram from the management of the New Theatre, Oxford, – 'Would you like to play date already booked with us. We have necessary permission.' The company was hastily reassembled, travelled to Oxford, opened as originally scheduled and played to good business. By mid-week the word had got around and next came a call from Theatre Royal, Hanley. 'What about working here next week, as previously fixed?' So on the following Sunday they travelled to Hanley in Staffordshire and opened to good business on the Monday. It got better and better through the week, and they were playing to full houses. On the Tuesday came a telephone call from the Stoll office, to say that a representative was on his way to see Sandy about the show going on to Bristol to play the Hippodrome, which was originally booked with Sandy for that week. However, when they got down to brass tacks, Stoll's apparently were not prepared to offer the usual terms. 'We will *hire* the theatre to you,' said the representative. 'You have been doing very well, if you do the same in Bristol you will make a packet.' Stoll of course, was playing it safe. Bristol, with its large dock area, was more of a priority target for the German bombers than Oxford or Hanley. After his week at Oxford and another obviously good one in prospect at Hanley, Sandy was feeling pretty confident, but nevertheless enquired cautiously, 'Well that depends on how much you want?'

'You can have the theatre, orchestra, staff, lighting and incidentals for five hundred pounds.' 'Right,' said Sandy, 'it's a deal!' Stolls immediately put on a big advertising campaign in Bristol, that Sandy with his great show was going to re-open the theatre. So when they got there on the Monday morning, Sandy found that the bookings were excellent, and in fact they had a tremendous week. He was feeling very jubilant when he got back to London after his trio of successful weeks in the provinces, and was delighted when his agent Mike Lyon told him that Sir Oswald Stoll wanted to see him, personally. 'But,' added Mike, 'I've a pretty good idea why he wants to see you, and if you take my advice, don't do it.'

'Don't do what?' enquired Sandy.

'I think he wants you to open the London Coliseum with your show, you'll lose your bootlaces, don't stand for it.'

'I've done very well up to now,' protested Sandy, 'I don't see why I couldn't do it in London.'

'Be it on your own head,' said Mike, 'I think you are making a mistake, but it's up to you.'

So, they went to see Sir Oswald. 'Sandy,' said the great man, 'you did a marvellous week at my theatre in Bristol. Why not come into London's West End and work a season at the Coliseum?' During this little talk, Mike Lyon, behind Sir Oswald's back, was shaking his head for a definite 'No'. Sandy ignored his signal and said 'Yes' to Sir Oswald's proposition. A moment after he gave his assent, he remembered with no little anxiety that the Coliseum was a very big theatre, where they usually presented lavish and costly bills. He enquired nervously, 'What about the bill, you don't expect me to fill it out with big-star names, do you?'

'Oh, no' replied Sir Oswald, 'I want exactly the same show as you had at Bristol.' So a contract was signed for *Can You Hear Me Mother?* to play a season at the London Coliseum. The show was advertised as a 'War-time Tonic – Laughs, Songs, Dances'. Because of the possibility of air raids, it was arranged that there would be two shows daily at 2 p.m. and 6 p.m. The show opened with a two o'clock matinee, but about half-past one the sirens howled out their warning message causing heart fluttering (up until now there were no air raids). As a result, hardly anyone turned up. Box-office receipts were about seventeen pounds and with prices at five shillings, three shillings and two shillings and sixpence, the audience could have been accommodated in one of Sir Oswald's super loos, a feature of the theatre. Further competition came in the way of the re-opening of the Palladium and other theatres. The moment it was announced that the Coliseum was opening up again, they did likewise. Bud Flanagan told Sandy that he and the rest of the cast went on half salary at the Palladium to help things out. Sandy carried on as best he could at the Coliseum, the artists worked hard even though working to small audiences. Some of the matinees were well patronised, the *Tatler* in its issue of the 15th November 1939 reported on *Can You Hear Me Mother?* thus:

This entertainment, featuring a comedian popular in the North, came quietly to the Coliseum and conquered the large family audience. Sandy Powell is an original, with a friendly approach and manner that is childlike and bland. His individuality gives pleasant relish to rather hackneyed material, whether he does a guest longing for a drink, an A.R.P. volunteer having fun with gas-masks and umbrellas, a glee singer unsure about his 'John Peel', a stage-box interrupter, or a coffee-stall keeper using the plates for xylophony with a pretty touch. The whole show, in fact, is pleasant. Other artists on the bill were Maisie Weldon (the late Harry Weldon's clever daughter), The Great Garcias who play Cornets and what-not while balancing on each others' heads, upside down and downside up, Vocalian Girls, Moonbeams, Saxophonists, stooges and accessory comedians.

At some of the performances Sandy brought his mother on stage, telling the audience that the Coliseum was the scene of her final performance before retirement, and she sang one of her old songs. Business generally in the West End theatres was very poor and during the third week Sandy asked to see Sir Oswald Stoll. 'I can't possibly afford to lose money on this scale,' he told him. 'The three weeks will cost me over two thousand pounds.' Sir Oswald listened sympathetically, saying that he was sorry it hadn't turned out as they had hoped.

'I'll release you from your contract of course,' he said, 'but what about opening next week at the Chiswick Empire. You should stand a better chance out there in the suburbs.' Sandy agreed, and this time Sir Oswald was right – they did a fantastic week's business.

Sandy had already moved his children, Peggy and Peter, to Blackpool, and thought it would be wiser to also get his expensive Buick up to what was hoped was a safer place. He had petrol for the journey, but the licence for the car had just run out, and, being a Yorkshireman, he thought that to buy a new licence for just one journey was a bit much. He'd just purchased a new licence for his small car and realised that it was similar in colour to a Guiness label. He steamed off a Guiness label from its bottle, cut it to shape and fixed it into the licence holder where it looked good.

Driving up to Blackpool, which was about two hundred and thirty miles from London, he got within a few miles of his destination when the car developed trouble and he stopped. A few moments afterwards, a passing car seeing him in trouble, pulled up, and out stepped two policeman. Sandy thought, 'This is it, here's where I'm for the high jump.' 'You all right sir?' they asked politely.

'Yes thank you,' replied Sandy, 'I know what the trouble is, I'll just push the car into the side of the road and soon fix it.'

'We'll give you a hand,' they replied, and proceeded to do so. Fortunately they didn't notice Sandy's discomfort, nor his faked licence and drove off little realising that they had let a 'desperate criminal' slip through their hands. Sandy got his breath back and vowed that he really wasn't cut out for crime.

One show that was doing well was *Shepherd's Pie* at the Prince's Theatre in London, and Mike Lyon suggested they see the show with a view to buying the rights for a provincial tour. They were delighted with what they saw; it was great entertainment with those fabulous comedians Sydney Howard and Arthur Riscoe playing the principal roles, the popular recording star Phyllis Robins, comedienne Vera Pierce, and character comedian and great all-round performer Richard Hearne. Sandy and Mike had a meeting with Firth Shepherd and came to terms with them for all rights of performance outside the West End of London. Moss Empires were happy to book the show. A strong cast was assembled with Sandy playing principal comic (the Sydney Howard part), Jack Edge, a great comedian who for many years had played lead in many West End revues and musical comedies (the Arthur Riscoe part), Margaret White (Vera Pierce role) and an up-and-coming young singer, Anne Lenner (in the Phyl Robbins part). The show opened at the Empire, Leeds, in March 1940, received a great reception and did a marvellous week's business. They did well also in Glasgow and Newcastle at the Empires there, but business slackened off with worrying news of the German invasion of Norway and Denmark, then Holland and Belgium. On 1st June the bulk of the British forces were evacuated at Dunkirk, with so many of their comrades being left behind. It was not a time for jollity, but of course the show went on. The company did a lot of hospital and troop shows while on tour. While playing the Edinburgh Empire, Sandy took his artists to Edinburgh Castle which had been turned into a Royal Air Force Hospital. Some of the airmen were in pretty poor shape, badly wounded and disfigured, and before the show, a young officer told Sandy, 'You know that we only have R.A.F. lads here, but there is one other boy, an airman, here, and our chaps would like him to see the show as well. He's a German who was brought down, and he's very badly hurt.' Sandy was very touched with the thought that, despite their own troubles, these R.A.F. boys were also concerned with a wounded enemy airman.

Sandy was also having trouble with his second comic, Jack Edge. He was a great performer, but a real 'shocker' for time. If he went well, he'd run over time and it was difficult to get him off the stage. When the audience were not very receptive, he did less than his scheduled time. Moss Empires were strict about timing of acts; their stage managers carefully noted the time played by each act, and these, together with comments about the act, were sent by theatre managers to head office in London. Val Parnell telephoned Sandy ordering him to tell Jack that he had to stick strictly to his allotted time, or get rid of him. Sandy explained that it was a bit difficult for him. Jack was a friend, they usually stayed at the same hotel while on tour, 'It's not an easy thing to do,' he said.

Parnell replied 'That's your problem, I'm talking about our theatres. If you allow this man to carry on in this way, it will effect business, so do something about it.' Sandy had a chat with Jack and things improved, but a little later, when they were working the Empire, Birmingham, it started all over again. He didn't turn up for one performance and Sandy found him still asleep at the hotel. Parnell got to hear about it and told Sandy, 'You must replace this man immediately, we will not allow this to go on any longer.' Sandy had to give Jack notice, not an easy thing to do to a friend and fellow artist, but it had to be done. Jack Edge did not speak to Sandy for many years after that episode. He obviously felt that it was Sandy's fault and not his own. Ernest Shannon the great impressionist was brought in to replace Jack. When the tour finished Sandy worked variety and also troop shows around the country to the army and air force. He remembers particularly a show held at an R.A.F. base on the East Coast. He got a great reception when he went on, but his act hardly got a laugh. He asked the stage manager, 'What's the matter with the audience – or was it me?'

He replied, 'I don't think many knew what you were talking about, they're Polish airmen.'

Sandy put together another show and they played quite a few dates, but with men being called up frequently, it became difficult, so Leslie Grade booked him for straight variety in which he did two or three spots on a bill for Moss Empires and Stoll's. At Golders Green Hippodrome, Leslie had put in an expensive bill. The bombing was very bad, consequently they did no business. Sandy and one or two of the other artists refused to take their full money – it would not have been fair on Leslie. For 1942 Sandy put together a very strong company and toured *Sandy Powell's Road Show*. The main supporting act was 'Harry Lester and his Hayseeds', 'The

A burlesque of the famous Brains Trust *with (left to right) Paul Thomson, Vincent Ryan, Alec Sanders and Sandy.*

Country Cousins' with Goofus and Arabella. The rest of the cast comprised singers, dancers and secondary comics who helped in the sketches. During the next few months, changes were made in the cast and Jack Demain came in to do this magic act which featured card and cigarette productions. Sandy who had been fascinated by conjurers ever since he was a lad, used to watch Jack's act every night and soon became familiar with every move. One night word came through that Edward Victor, the shadowgraph artist, had been taken ill and could not appear. The show being an act short, Sandy asked Jack Demain for permission to burlesque a few of his tricks. Jack agreed, and from then on Sandy followed Jack's act with his own burlesqued version. Sandy further developed the idea and it eventually became one of his classics. It is still one of the most requested items in Sandy's programme today.

Val Parnell never missed an opportunity to pull Sandy's leg about his 'little show' whenever he played a Moss date. 'Why don't you find another Peter Kane like you did at Liverpool before the war. His wasn't an act, but at least it was a big name.' At that time the 'Brains Trust' – Lady Astor, Professor Joad, Julian Huxley, Commander Campbell and Question Master Donald McCullough – were great favourites of the public. Sandy liked the Commander best of all and he said to Mike Lyon, 'It would be great if we could get Commander Campbell in our show.'

Mike replied, 'Well let's ask him, he can only say "No".' Mike got in touch with the Brains Trust producer and received an invitation to see the great radio team at work. There was no studio audience, just Mike and Sandy sitting quietly in the corner. The team worked very efficiently and Sandy was very amused when, after the show, he heard Lady Astor accuse the Professor of 'stealing one of her lines'. It was quite a bitter exchange and it reminded him of comics having a row about gags in a show. They talked to the Commander about their idea but he was doubtful about the feasibility of him fitting into a music-hall bill. He was finally persuaded to give it a try for a six-week stint at two hundred pounds a week. Commander Campbell's first week was at the Nottingham Empire where he was billed as 'The famous personality of The Brains Trust'. Sandy introduced him to the audience and the Commander, a wonderful talker, told how he became a member of the team and also about the other members of the panel. He then recited Rudyard Kipling's poem 'If', spoke about his life in the Merchant and Royal Navy and finished his act with a monologue of his own composition about the Merchant Navy. Sandy had helped him to arrange his act and it went down very well at Nottingham, but the following week at the Hackney Empire, it did not register. However, his name on the bill caused a good deal of talk and when he got more confident about working on a stage, his act improved and always received big applause at the finish. Sandy, unable to resist the temptation of doing a burlesque, very quickly (with permission) followed the Commander's act with a short version of his own.

When the Commander left the show eventually, Sandy put on a bois-terous 'Brains Trust' scene with himself as Commander Dumbell, Paul Thomson as 'Julian Juxley', Alec Sanders as 'Professor Toad', and Vincent Ryan as the Question Master. It soon developed into one of the strongest items in Sandy's ever-widening repertoire of sketches. The replacement for the Commander was Harry Hemsley, impersonator of children's voices and one of the big radio and music-hall favourites of the day. He was later replaced by the great protean artist, Owen McGiveny, whose amazing act was the playing of all the characters in a one-man drama from Dickens. It wasn't long before Sandy had dreamt up a burles-que of McGiveny's act. Getting his permission for the use of his set and also to do a burlesque take-off immediately after the serious version had taken its well-earned applause, he brought to maturity the best of all his burlesques.

Another great comedy item was introduced to Sandy by Harry Lester; this was the 'Throwing Axe' stunt that Harry had been using in his shows since the early twenties. In 1915, when quite a young man, Harry Lester came to this country from America, and made his first appearance at the Victoria Palace with his father John and brother Burton in a family act. Originating in Fort Worth, Texas, they had trouped with Wild-West shows and circus and also worked in Vaudeville. Just before coming to Britain they had worked through Australia and South Africa. They put on many new and novel acts over the years, like 'The 'Frisco Five', the first of the Jazz bands, 'The Cowboy Syncopators', 'The Midget's Circus', and many revues of their own. 'Harry Lester and His Hayseeds', the act that worked with Sandy for a long time, was a headliner on the music halls and appeared in the Royal Variety Performance at the London Palladium in 1946. So the 'Throwing Axe' stunt that he did with Sandy had a long history of authen-ticity and experience behind it. The props consisted of a large, solid wooden board with a hinged frame at the back so that it could stand almost up-right, like an easel. The cowboy, an overbearing, dominating, bullying type persuaded the comedian to stand in front of the board as a deputy for the usual assistant, to act as a 'target' for the axe-throwing cowboy. Harry said that it was very difficult to get comics to do this stunt with him. In the first *Lester Revue* in 1923, they had the great comedy pair 'Farr and Farland' in the show. Harry did the stunt with Chick Farr, an upper-class-ninny-dude character, who got screams of laughter as the reluctant target. But in later shows other comics with whom Harry worked were not par-ticularly funny and the gag failed. One confessed to Harry that he was scared: 'I've got a wife and two kids to think about.'

Sandy wanted to go abroad to work in front of the troops so he went to ENSA Headquarters at Drury Lane and saw one of their chief executives, Greatorex Newman. 'What do you want to do, Sandy?' he asked. 'Have a good time or do something less comfortable and more useful, like going to the places where the boys can do with seeing a star of your calibre?'

The Road Show of 1942 *at the Alhambra, Bradford, with Harry Lester and his Hayseeds.*

'That's for me,' replied Sandy.

'Fine,' said Greatorex. 'What about working out from Cairo?' And with Sandy's reply of 'Yes', he advised him to get some tropical kit. Sandy and his wife Katie were next called for innoculations and in February 1944, they reported to Drury Lane one dark night. It was all very hush-hush. They got together with the other members of the company – Billy Scott-Coomber, vocalist and compere; Jeannette Haley, soprano; and the two St John sisters. In total darkness they were shepherded to a waiting blacked-out charabanc which whisked them off to a blacked-out station, then into a blacked-out train crowded with Canadian soldiers who were standing in the corridors. Fortunately seats had been reserved for the company, and they sat for hours in the dark, travelling by fits and starts, not knowing where they were going. Eventually they reached their destination; a station Sandy recognised as Glasgow. Then they were driven to some docks they presumed was Greenock, from where they travelled by ship – the *Almonzora*. The ship was crammed full; soldiers were sleeping on deck, in fact anywhere and everywhere. There were no cabins available, and the artists were fixed up with make-shift accommodation. Sandy and his wife were given a curtained-off section of a gangway. Food was plentiful but served up in a rough and ready way, and there wasn't a drink in sight. When they were well under way, Sandy discovered that their destination was Italy – not Egypt as they had been told. When they finally disembarked it was at Naples. On their second day there they were given a large army truck and a driver who told them that they were bound for the Adriatic coast on the other side of Italy. It was hardly a luxury trip, petrol tins were used for seating and they hadn't been on the road long when they ran into a snow storm. Sandy thought wryly of the tropical clothes they had been advised to take and were packed in their suitcase. They huddled together in an effort to get warm when conditions worsened, and on one stretch of the road it took them four and a half hours to cover seventeen miles. Saddle-sore, hungry and thirsty, they arrived at Termoli and pulled up at a Canadian camp site. They received a warm welcome and were given a good meal. They were then sent on their way with a supply of tinned food and a couple of bottles of 'warming-up' liquid. Sandy cannot speak too highly of this friendly Canadian hospitality. Another long haul took them to Vasto where they were due to give a show the following evening. Michael Brennan, the actor, was the ENSA officer in charge. 'What can I do for you?' he asked.

'After that journey, we need some food and a couple of bottles of Scotch for a start; after that somewhere we can get a wash and a soft bed to sleep on.'

Michael replied, 'I am afraid that things are not too good here, the Germans are bombing the town and keep putting out the lights. Also water is rationed to one pint per person per day. You can either wash, shave or make tea with it, it's up to you.' They were too tired to argue so they tumbled into bed and were soon asleep. The next morning they looked at themselves in the mirror and decided that, although they did not look too good, they needed a cup of tea much more than a wash. In fact they remained fairly unwashed during the next couple of days. A local theatre was the venue for their show and with a packed audience out front, Billy Scott-Coomber did the opening warm-up spot and then went into a big build-up speech: 'It's now my pleasure to introduce one of our biggest stars, a man who had come thousands of miles to entertain you, the one and only Sandy Powell!'

As Sandy walked on to terrific applause, every light in the building went out. A German bomb had dropped nearby and blacked them out. Although naturally scared, Sandy had the professional presence of mind to call out into the darkness, 'That's a hell of a welcome!' The big laugh that followed gave him and the audience time to settle and he called out, 'What shall we do, lads, carry on in the dark or pack up and try again tomorrow?'

'Carry on,' they yelled back, and one of the men brought out a torch and shone it on to the stage.

'That's an idea,' said Sandy, 'Can anybody else oblige me with a light?' Many of them obliged by shining their torches, so Sandy cracked gags and they carried on by torch-light. Soon candles were produced and set up as footlights, and it turned out to be a fabulous night enjoyed as much by the performers as by the lads out front.

The next move was to Lanciano a few miles north and quite close to the firing line; the Germans were only a couple of miles away. Lanciano, was a very beautiful city and in the Middle Ages had been one of the chief trading centres of Italy. The company gave shows in the lovely old Opera House which was well within shelling distance by the Germans. One of the officers took them to the gun sites; he invited Sandy to fire a shell at the Germans. 'I'd sooner sing to them than try to blow 'em up,' said Sandy, 'that would punish them more.' The officer also took them to see a road that was nick-named 'The Mad Mile'. This ran parallel to the German lines and through his binoculars Sandy could see the British racing along the road on motor cycles. It was a sort of 'dare' for them. 'Sooner them than me,' said Sandy. Doing shows every day under these conditions was a bit nerve-racking. They lived in a sort of boarding-house: many of the rooms had alcoves in which was set a figure of the Madonna, and the only food served up was tinned corned beef. Sandy enquired, 'Can you do something else with it; cook it, boil it, or anything else?' When they answered, 'No' he replied, more in sorrow than in anger: 'Well try painting it for a change!'

One night they were invited to the Officers' Mess, and a young officer sat at the piano playing softly a tune that Sandy thought was beautiful. He asked, 'What are you playing?'

'It's a German song,' replied the officer. 'They play it on their radio and it's very popular with our chaps. It's called "Lily Marlene".' That was the first time Sandy heard the tune that became a classic among war-time melodies.

On the last night their show was cancelled. 'It's getting a bit too close, it would be wiser for you to get moving.' So they packed up and made their way back to Vasto, and not too soon, because the day after they left, one of the German shells landed right in the middle of the square in which the Opera House stood, and the theatre was badly damaged. Back in Vasto, Michael Brennan found them a coach and driver to take them back to Naples. It was an enormous Italian vehicle equipped with spacious luxury sleeping quarters and dining and sitting areas.

The return journey was much more comfortable, and travelling through the villages, the local population and the soldiers greeted them with whistles and cheers, which they duly acknowledged with pleasure and enthusiasm. Nevertheless they found it most puzzling. The mystery was cleared up later when they were informed that their luxury coach was normally used as a travelling brothel. Its purpose was to take the girls to the front line! A week playing to the troops at the Opera House in Naples was followed by a run down to Sorrento to entertain the troops in that area. Accommodation was at an hotel right on the sea front, and in the early hours of one morning Sandy was awakened by the noise of heavy bombardment. They went out and looked across the bay to Naples which was being raided. The noise and excitement lasted all night and prevented the possibility of any sleep, and Sandy, not normally a heavy smoker, smoked a great deal, so much so that he was taken ill with a bout of bronchitis and the doctor insisted that he took at least two weeks off to get over it. He recommended going to the beautiful island of Iskia a few miles out in the Bay of Naples. While they were there the Cassino offensive was in full swing and although they were over fifty miles away, they could hear the noise of the guns and aerial bombardment. Back again with the company in Naples, they gave a show on the warship *Boxer*.

During the evening a signal came through asking Sandy to go to Australia to be the first British celebrity to appear there since the war started. The ENSA representative was somebody that Sandy knew very well, Harold Mellor, who used to be manager of the Palace, Blackpool. He said that he would make all the necessary arrangements, but insisted that the matter be kept strictly secret. There was no commercial transport available, the army or navy would have to get them there and back. Eventually they got away on the *Warwick Castle*. There were no other passengers on the ship and each member of the company had a cabin to themselves, Sandy being given a first-class luxury suite to share with his wife. One morning they were anchored off a coast that looked familiar to Sandy – he was sure they were lying off Algiers since he'd seen it when doing a North African cruise before the war. 'Where are we?' he enquired of an officer, 'Surely this isn't the way to Australia?'

The officer laughed and said, 'We are bound for the U.K., if you want to get to Australia, you are on the wrong ship.' An urgent message was sent ashore to ask that the local ENSA representative come aboard, and when he did Sandy recognised him to be the famous actor Nigel Patrick. 'We are supposed to be doing a six weeks' tour of Australia and then return to the U.K. I've got to get back to fulfill some important engagements.'

'There is nothing here I can fix to get you to Australia,' replied Patrick. 'The best thing you can do in these circumstances is to leave this ship and let me fill in your time here in North Africa. There are not many British troops here, but they would very much like to see you, and there are plenty of American troops who would also welcome your show.'

As there did not seem to be an alternative, Sandy gladly accepted. They were installed in the luxurious Aletti Hotel, the best in Algiers, in which the Americans had set up their headquarters. At dinner that night, Sandy noticed the glamorous Marlene Dietrich sitting at the next table, looking very beautiful dressed in her smartly cut American khaki uniform, also the famous coloured French singer Josephine Baker. Both these great artists were there to entertain the American troops. Sandy's first show was to several hundred British troops at a place called Blida situated right on the edge of the Sahara. He remembers it well because, as he says, 'It was so blida hot.' Then followed a tour along the North African coast to Annaba (Bone), Tunis, Tripoli, then back to Algiers and down to the west-coast base at Dakar where they got word to prepare to go back to Rome which was in the process of being liberated. On the way they gave shows in Casablanca and heard that the Allied Forces had landed in France and the liberation of Europe had started.

The company then made their way to Italy, while Sandy and his wife, with the kind cooperation of the American authorities were put on a plane that touched down especially for their benefit, at Gibraltar. They were the only civilians on the plane, the rest of the passengers being American soldiers on their way to a place of detention. At Gibraltar they found an ENSA officer who managed to get them on the mail plane bound for U.K. Back in their flat in Russell Square, they were soon given a taste of the new terror that was hitting London. They had been told about this new weapon – a pilotless plane filled with explosive, which came down when its engine stopped. That night they heard the sound of a plane, its engine stopped and they waited in terror for the climax. It came with a terrific explosion, the lights went out and so did every pane of glass in the flat. Thankful at being alive and unhurt, they went into the street and the air-raid warden told them that the 'Doodle Bug' had landed right in the centre of Russell Square, in an open space. It was a narrow squeak!

The very next morning Sandy went to Drury Lane to offer his services to work abroad again for the forces. He thought: 'If the Germans are after me, I might as well be doing something useful at the time.'

A super company was formed comprising Sandy, Flanagan and Allen, Florence Desmond, Kay Cavendish, the pianist, and Billy Scott-Coomber. The arrangements, time and point of departure were kept very quiet. A few days later came a call from the 'Lane' to attend there that evening. 'What's it all about? asked Sandy.

'Sorry, we cannot tell you the reason, but there is no need for you to bring anything special, just come as you are.' At Drury Lane that night the company was put into a large coach and driven down through South London,

A sight for any tired soldier's eyes! Roy Jeffries with Sandy in the amusing 'Air Force Woman' sketch.

Surrey and into Sussex through country lanes and eventually arrived at a big house. They hadn't any idea as to where they were. It looked like a large country mansion presumably taken over for military purposes. A civilian gentleman greeted and then ushered them into a large room in which were stacks and stacks of steel helmets. Each person was fitted for size, and their helmet labelled and put on one side. The company were politely thanked, taken out to the coach and driven back to Drury Lane where they arrived in the early hours of the morning. The fitting of steel helmets seemed to be the sole object of this extraordinary operation. They were sent home with instructions to stand-by for the call. Then followed a further call to Drury Lane, again at night, and they were driven in a coach to a sort of security quarantine place 'somewhere in Sussex'. The next day they were kitted-out with officers' battle dress and overcoat. Sandy slept in a tent that night, and the next night they were taken to Newhaven where they boarded a landing craft and set sail for France. The women were taken across by ship.

The landing craft was packed with soldiers who seemed in great spirits. Sandy and Bud led the boys in singing popular choruses nearly all the way across, stopping only when a plane flew overhead. In the faint light of dawn they saw hundreds of small craft waiting their turn to enter Mulberry Harbour. It was an unforgettable sight. When they landed on the Normandy beach there was nobody to meet them. But they hardly expected a reception committee, so they sat on boxes they found scattered around. There was plenty of activity but of course the military were too busy to worry about a bunch of actors. Eventually an ENSA officer turned up with two Jeeps which whisked them away to Bayeaux, where they were to meet up with their female colleagues. Bayeux was crowded with troops, all on the move. Billeted in an empty house, Sandy and Bud shared a large room and Ches and Billy the other, although there wasn't a pane of glass left in the place, which made it very cold. During the next couple of days they were taken to see the German fortifications which had been stormed at great cost by our troops. Then came their first show which took place at British H.Q. in the open air and to an audience who seemed to be predominantly officers. Afterwards the champagne flowed freely and Sandy had the feeling that this was going to be the sort of thing they would be doing – the stars of music hall entertaining the military officers and gentlemen, and that wasn't his idea of 'entertaining the troops'. So he and Billy Scott-Coomber went off on their own and joined up with a small ENSA group, a straight singer, comic, and six girl dancers.

Between them they arranged a good programme. They made their way to Flers, which had been the scene of heavy fighting and was now just a mass of rubble, got hold of the ENSA officer who provided them with a large sleeper-wagon and driver, and they drove off looking for troops to entertain. They were directed to some barracks but when they got there the place was deserted, the troops had moved on. Moving on they gave shows wherever there were troops to play to – mainly in the fields. When they arrived at Caen they found the place in a mess; the audiences were small because the soldiers were either chasing the Germans or clearing up the mess. They continued doing as much as they could and eventually they rolled into Paris on 3rd September, just ten days after the liberation. There was great excitement and their caravan was greeted enthusiastically by the Parisians who stopped them frequently and insisted that they take wine with them. The next day they restocked and drove off on the return journey working their way back to the coast. Just outside Rouen they came across a British soldier who told them that his regiment was stationed nearby and Sandy asked whether the troops would like to see their show. 'Funny you should say that,' said the soldier, 'we have a concert party of our own and we are putting on a show tonight. It's not professional, but we do our best.'

'What about joining forces,' suggested Sandy. And that's what they did, and had a marvellous evening. Working where they could, the company travelled to the coast through towns and villages some of which were flattened almost completely.

In France for just over six weeks, Sandy thought that perhaps it was too soon after the landing for entertainment to have been properly organised. But their efforts had brought pleasure to the troops, and Sandy has the memory of being there at a historic moment. His next personal problem was to get back to England to fulfil some important dates that had been booked. Fortunately he managed to get fixed up, and the rest of the company stayed on in France and continued with the good work.

After the war, troop shows continued in one form or another. The *News of the World* sponsored their 'V' (for Victory) shows in Germany, laid on a Dakota aircraft and paid all the expenses and overheads, including the artists. In Berlin, a city that seemed in ruins, they worked in a cinema. The company included Roy Rich and Brenda Bruce as comperes, and supporting Sandy were Kenway & Young, Sirdani, Beryl Orde, Mary Honri, Sara Gregory, Kay and Ankers and the 'Strolling Vagabond', Cavan O'Connor. As so often happens with this type of show, trouble arises when the running order is being arranged. In music hall an act goes on in the spot allocated to it – no argument. In this instance nobody wanted to go on first, they weren't keen on 'closing' either. Out came all the usual excuses: 'I'm a singer, it's too early for me to go on,' or 'That's a shocking spot to do magic'. They quibbled until Sandy (who was the biggest 'name' on the bill) said, 'Don't worry, I'll go on first turn and I'll close the show as well.' He opened the bill to an audience of British soldiers and got a terrific reception. They were the first artists they had seen, so the first on had the most applause! Sandy did several shows in Germany to the occupation troops, travelling on the autobahn by coach. On another trip the beautiful singer Yana was a big hit as was also the Australian comedian Terry Scanlon. This tour was more extensive, and covered Holland as well as Germany. Combined Services Entertainment (C.S.E.) took up where ENSA left off, and they organised entertainment for the troops stationed around the world.

His first tour with them was all around the Eastern end of the Mediterranean with a five-handed company that included his wife Kay and Dicky

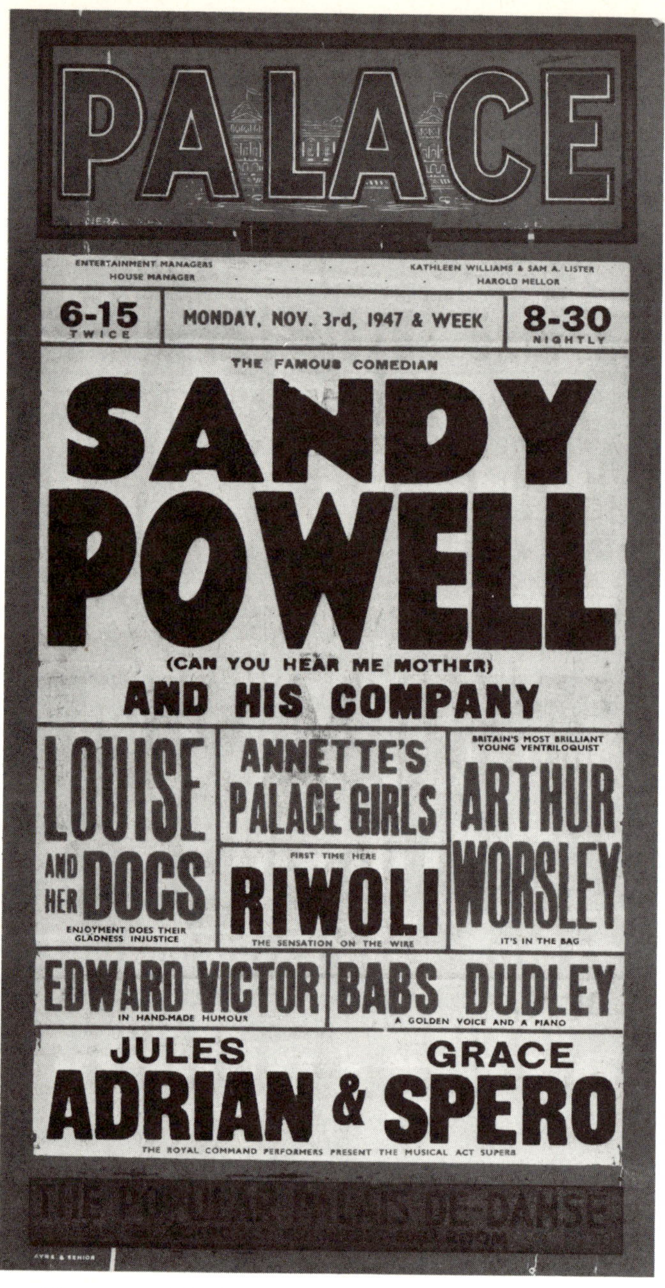

The Palace Theatre at Blackpool proclaims its stars for 3 November 1947. The writing of the descriptive puffs which appear under the artistes' names was a minor art. Who could resist an act with the runner, ENJOYMENT DOES THEIR GLADNESS INJUSTICE? *Or* IN HAND-MADE HUMOUR? *Today these gentle confidences have been replaced by the hard-sell of press-agentry staggering under its own weight of hyperbole.*

Dawson (who married Diana Dors) a good working and very happy group. Their first scheduled stop was at Valetta in Malta, but they nearly didn't make it; the plane almost came down in the sea during a very rough flight. However, they played many shows during a two weeks stay on the island. The next stop was Tripoli, then along the coast, which had been the scene of so much fighting in the war, to Benghazi, Derna and Tobruk (some places for only two nights, others a week) the Canal Zone camps at Port Fuad, Ismailia and Suez and then on to Cyprus, spending Christmas in Nicosia, then working around the island for just over six weeks – Famagusta, Limassol, Kyrenia, Paphos and Larnaca. These were troublesome times and they were not too sorry to fly off to Nairobi in Kenya.

The troupe spent three weeks in Nairobi in a hotel and, using it as a base, toured camps in the out-lying areas, including some that were right on the Equator. Sandy says 'I wasn't too cool.' Aden was the next stop where they played in an open-air theatre. But things weren't easy there and they beat a hasty retreat on a plane going to Khartoum. They were now off-schedule, but as Sandy had discovered in travelling around, a little goodwill and friendliness will take you a long way. So, applying this axiom to their difficult situation, he managed to 'work their passage' on a circuitous journey back to the U.K. It had been a long and arduous trip, but one well worth doing. One of Sandy's happy memories was a show at a camp where troops from different theatres of war were assembled for sorting out. 'They were a glorious audience,' says Sandy, 'most of them had come from places where they never had a sight of a show.' When they finished around eleven o'clock at night, the C.O. went on stage to thank the artists in the usual effusive way, but the audience wouldn't listen and kept yelling for more. 'Do you want more?' asked Sandy. 'Yes,' they yelled back, 'start again.' So they did another complete show! Speeches of thanks were usually lengthy and embarrassing in exaggerated praise. The best Sandy ever experienced was at an American Base. At the end of a most successful show, a young C.O. went on stage, pointed to the artists and said to his soldiers 'Give!' And they did, a great response to the briefest and best speech of thanks he had ever heard.

8

Third Time Lucky

ROMANCE first came into Sandy's life when he worked in his first pantomime. A pretty young girl called Katie Hughes caught his eye and heart. Twice nightly he watched her act; she was a vivacious performer and danced and sang a ragtime number called 'I'm Going Down South.' During the run of the show they became sweethearts – an innocent courtship – since Sandy was a very shy young man. At the end of the tour they parted but exchanged vows to keep in touch with each other. Eventually, however, they went their own theatrical ways and, as so often happens in the business, they did not manage to get together again.

During the early twenties while working in variety at the Hippodrome, Nottingham, Sandy met a pretty young girl called Peggy Whitty. Sandy was one of three variety acts that made up the first half of the programme, and Peggy was in a revue called 'Stock Pot' which filled the second half of the bill. They became good friends and kept in touch with each other when touring in different shows. They came together again, and eventually married. Peggy worked with Sandy in variety and then in the *Sandy and His Pals* show on tour. During the following years they had two lovely children: first a girl they called Peggy and a year later a boy, Peter. Life was good at first, but then came the period when Sandy was busy filming, broadcasting, and touring round. Things started going awry domestically. They separated during the filming of *It's a Grand Old World* and the two children stayed with Sandy.

His solicitor told him that the other side had engaged as counsel Mr Gilbert Beyfus, one of the big legal guns of the day. 'He's a big star,' commented Sandy. 'A very big star,' replied his solicitor. 'There is only one man better in divorce proceedings, he will cost you a lot of money, but it will be well worth it – Sir Patrick Hastings.'

Sir Patrick Hastings was booked to top Sandy's bill of divorce and as second top to Sir Patrick they booked Russell Vick, who was later to become an eminent Queen's Counsel. Sandy had booked a good bill. There was naturally a lot of Fleet Street activity and publicity; Sandy's was a household name and the prospect of theatrical dirty-linen being washed in public was a mouth-watering attraction for some of the newshounds and their scandal-loving readers. The first day of the hearing at the Law Courts in the Strand attracted a big house. At a music hall, the 'house-full' boards, would have been put out. That night two people were featured on the front page of the *Evening News*. Says Sandy: 'The other man got top billing, but I couldn't complain about being second top because the other fellow was Hitler!'

The legal giants battled it out for five whole days. On the first morning, Sandy, although he had an excellent case, and contrary to the opinion of his legal advisers, was anxious to keep it out of court and insisted on settlement terms being offered. The offer was turned down. As the trial progressed, the other side said they would agree, but by this time it was becoming evident that Sandy's case was so strong that his counsel was winning hands down. Sandy says Sir Patrick was a great performer: 'His timing was immaculate.' The cut and thrust between the lawyers went on remorselessly throughout the trial, and on the final day Sir Patrick was at his very best. He used his brief to punctuate and emphasise the important words in his speech by slapping the papers on the palm of his hand to get the full effect. 'It was a lovely piece of business,' says Sandy, 'It was timed to perfection.' 'Here,' he thundered, 'is a man greatly beloved by his fellow professionals, a man who delights the children with his wonderful and sympathetic work in pantomime. A man who is known the length and breadth of the land for shows that are clean, healthy, family entertainment,

Katie Hughes, Sandy's first sweetheart and second wife.

and you are trying to damage his future.' As he said the word 'future', he slapped the papers sharply on his hand, then spread his arms wide in a dramatic gesture – and threw the papers right into the face of Sandy who was sitting just behind.

A few hours later the verdict was given in Sandy's favour with damages of two thousand pounds awarded to him. The other side was ordered to pay the entire cost of the action. The total sum involved was twelve thousand pounds, but the other side did not have a bean, so Sandy footed the bill as it wasn't in his heart to be vindictive. As he remarked later: 'Putting a show on in the West End of London is always a bit of a gamble. This one ran for five days. The stars were on a big salary, it was an expensive bill, and although the "theatre" was large, its capacity was small, so it was bound to cost a bit of brass.' Sandy did not bear any grudge and, during the following years, occasional telephone calls were made between him and his divorced wife. But, his life had been made very difficult at a time, when, ironically, he was at his peak professionally. He says that it will remain a mystery to him, how he coped with his problems. 'I was lucky,' he says, 'in having good friends to help me through.' He was earning a large sum of money which he could not enjoy because of the constant worry about his domestic affairs. He got over it by working hard at the profession he loved. Sandy was, and still is completely stage-struck.

A piano and a ukulele and the White Sisters, Kay and Ida.

One night in 1939, soon after the war started, when Sandy re-opened the London Coliseum with his show *Can You Hear Me Mother?* the stagedoor keeper told him that a young lady wanted to see him. The girl, about eighteen years old, looked amazingly like his first sweetheart, Katie Hughes. 'My name is Irene,' said the girl, 'I believe you knew my mother.'

'If her name is Katie, I certainly did know her,' replied Sandy. Irene told Sandy all about her mother and her sister, Joan. Katie's marriage was apparently on the rocks. Following this meeting, Sandy and Katie met and, not long after, he found himself in a divorce action that was quickly and quietly settled. In 1942, they married and settled in a flat in Whitley Court, Russell Square. The flat was large enough to allow the two girls to live with them. Sandy was working hard in all kinds of shows; for the forces, variety and broadcasting. Katie travelled around with him and they returned home whenever possible. The girls found jobs, but these were troubled times and what with the bombing, and the pressures of living in the West End, they found the situation difficult to handle. Katie, anxious not to burden Sandy with domestic troubles again, had many quarrels with her daughters. She was away with Sandy a good deal for his forces shows and also assisted him in variety. But on their return there were always problems, and, becoming more and more distressed each time, Katie was at breaking point. Sandy was away working up North when he was sent word to return immediately. Katie was in University Hospital desperately ill. She lingered for five days but the doctors couldn't save her and she died on 7th December 1947.

Sandy was shocked. It was coming up to pantomime time and he was booked to play the Opera House, Blackpool, and rehearsals were scheduled to start a few days after the funeral. He went to see his friend Bert Montague. 'I don't think I can make it, Bert,' he said. 'Doing panto after what I've been through will be more than I can manage.'

Bert replied, 'Sandy, the best way to forget is to work, as hard as you can. Don't moon around. Work is the answer, believe me.' Sandy took his advice, and thanks to the help of his colleagues, particularly George Bolton, managed to carry on.

Following this pantomime Sandy went back into variety. He remembers it well because the weather was awful in 'the year of the snows'. He needed a woman for his sketches. 'Any ideas?' he asked his agent Mike Lyon.

After some thought, Mike said, 'I think I can get you the ideal person. Kay White, an excellent performer. Do you know her?' Sandy didn't and it was left that Mike would arrange a meeting.

Actually Mike could not have thought of a better person. Kay had come from a wonderful theatrical background. Her mother, Katie Thorburn, had been one of the legendary 'Gaiety Girls', and her uncle was Charles Thorburn, a famous performer with the D'Oyley Carte Company playing in Gilbert and Sullivan Opera's at the Savoy Theatre during the end of the last century. So Kay and her elder sister Ida had been taught dancing and singing, and when it was found that Kay had a great aptitude for the piano, she was encouraged to work hard at it. At the age of fifteen Kathleen White

Kay White in her first sketch with Sandy, 'The Return'.

became a 'Cochran Girl' a dancer in the Corps de Ballet, together with Greta Fayne (who later became a film star), Phyllis Cardew, Queenie Robertson, Edith Timmis and Rene Mowbray in *League of Notions* at The New Oxford Theatre, London. Their cast included the fabulous Dolly Sisters, the comedian A. W. Baskcombe, the beautiful Evelyn Laye, the California Mocking Bird, Margaret McKee, and 'Tex' MacLeod. It was a thrilling experience for so young a girl. Kathleen (Kay) White worked in many other Cochran shows with girls who were later to become famous; for example, Anna Neagle, Florence Desmond and Jessie Matthews. Kay and sister Ida formed an act, 'The White Sisters', billed as 'Harmonised Singers, Pianist and Speciality Dancers', and joined Mr R. B. Salisbury's Musical and Comedy Company in *The Blue Train*, a new musical comedy which had enjoyed great success at the Prince of Wales Theatre in London. They toured South Africa, India and the Far East. In the company were artists who were later famous, including Frances Day, Gordon Rennie and George Curzon. On their return they played in Felgate King and Elsie Mayfair's *Revels* on the Pier at Eastbourne. Then they went into variety, featuring songs written and composed by Kay. The sisters broke up, quite amicably and Kay went into pantomime as Cinderella, a role she later played in fourteen productions.

By the time Mike Lyon contacted her she was tired of touring and had retired from the business. She and her younger sister Floris opened a dancing school at home in Lewisham, London. Floris also had had experience in shows and with Kay's long and very varied experience, they were well-qualified to train pupils in dance technique and performance. So if Mike could pull it off and persuade Kay, Sandy, had the possibility of getting a really first-class, all-round artist to join him, although at the time he had never heard of Kay White.

Mike didn't find things as easy as he had hoped. He telephoned Kay and said: 'I want you to do me a personal favour, darling.'

'Mike,' she replied, 'if it's what I think it is, forget it. I'm now out of the business and doing very nicely thank you. So if it is a job you are offering, it is no use.'

Unabashed by this unequivocal refusal, Mike said sweetly, 'You must be a mind-reader, love, but, please hear me out. A very good friend of mine is in dead trouble. He is a very nice person called Sandy Powell and he is in desperate need for a woman feed just for a couple of weeks while I fix him with someone permanent. Do it for me as a personal favour.'

Kay replied, 'Mike, you have been very helpful to me in the past and I would love to help you, but Floris and I have just started a dancing school. It is going very well and this would be a very awkward time for me to get away.'

'At least come up here and meet him,' begged Mike. 'He's really a very good sort, is opening at the Palace, Bath, on Monday, and you are the only person who could help him out in this emergency.' Kay reluctantly agreed to meet Sandy in Mike's office, and found Sandy as nice as Mike had said

Kay and Sandy Powell as they are today.

he was. After a long chat, Mike suggested a salary of fifteen pounds a week to which Kay agreed but emphasised that it must be for two weeks only, not a minute more. Kay and Sandy left together and he invited her to have a drink with him at the nearby Trocadero Restaurant, a favourite show-business rendezvous in Shaftesbury Avenue just by Piccadilly Circus. Kay found Sandy a good listener and very interested in what she told him about herself and her mother, who had been in the business before her. As they got up to leave, Sandy asked: 'As time is short, would it be possible for you to rehearse with me today. My place is only a few minutes from here and I'm sure that my manager Bert Murfin will be able to fix us up with a spot of lunch.' Coming from someone as modest and nice as she thought Sandy was, Kay judged that it wasn't one of those casting-couch propositions she had had from some of the agents to whom she had applied for work over the years. So she wasn't surprised when it turned out to be as Sandy had said. They had a good rehearsal and lunch with Bert Murfin, who proved to be a good cook.

Back in Lewisham Kay had quite a job explaining it all to Floris who said, 'I told you so', but nevertheless promised to hold the fort while Kay was away. Another rehearsal and lunch followed the next day and a couple of days later they opened at the Palace, Bath, in Somerset. The first sketch Kay played in was about a soldier coming home on leave, called 'The Return', and it went very well on opening night, as did all the other pieces she did in the show. She enjoyed getting back on the stage and she realised that Sandy was a very shy, nervous and kindly man. Towards the end of the first house, Sandy became a little more relaxed, happy in the knowledge that in Kay he had a competent performer. Towards the end of the week, Bert knocked on Kay's door: 'Sandy wonders if you'd like a drink with him after the show?'

'Certainly,' she replied and when the curtain came down they had a drink in his dressing-room and after a while Bert drove them home dropping Kay off at her digs on the way.

The weather was shocking when they arrived in Folkestone for the next week's engagement at the Pleasure Gardens Theatre. A freeze-up brought electricity cuts and performances had to be fixed for 4 p.m. and the second house at 6.30 p.m. Despite the bad weather, they did quite a good week's business, and Kay and Sandy were getting on very well. So much so that when Sandy enquired whether she would be kind enough to stay on for another two weeks at the Empire, Leeds, and then Portsmouth, Kay didn't have the heart to say 'no,' and so it went on. When it became obvious that Kay was going to stay with the show, the dancing school was put completely in the hands of Floris, who by this time had become quite reconciled to the arrangement.

Kay became Sandy's right arm. Not only did she perform in the sketches but was also concerned with the production and choreography of the various *Sandy Powell Road Shows* during the following years. In 1951 they were married at the Marylebone Register Office in London. Sandy's family

– Lily and his children, Peggy and Peter – took Kay to their hearts.

The honeymooners made for Paris but when they unpacked they found their travellers cheques had been left behind. Soon getting through their English currency, they had to wait for funds to come through from England. Walking along the Champs-Elysées, Sandy remarked to Kay: 'Isn't it marvellous, when I'm in England, South Africa or New Zealand, hardly a day goes without somebody or the other coming up to me and saying, "Can you hear me, Mother?". Now, when we need someone like that from whom we could borrow a few francs, it doesn't happen.' Actually the manager of the hotel was happy to oblige.

In 1958 they bought a house in Eastbourne, just a stone's throw from the pier where for so many years Sandy had reigned supreme. Sandy and Kay are inseparable: wherever Sandy is, at his side is Kay. 'Kay is a marvellous wife. It's just like the old gag in which the wife says, "I'm leaving", and the husband replies, "Good, I'll come with you." If Kay left here the whole place would fall down, she does everything.'

9

Mr. Eastbourne

THE first time Sandy appeared on the Pier at Eastbourne was in nineteen thirty-six. He was 'Star Guest Artist' in a Sunday Concert presented by Clarkson Rose, whose summer show *Twinkle* had run there for nine seasons. When the Second World War erupted, every show in the country closed down by government orders. The Pier Company promised 'Clarkie' that when the war ended he could return to the pier with his show. But, when peace came, they asked him to work in the theatre at the sea-end of the pier. 'Clarkie' who had always worked in the Pavilion at the land-end, near the entrance to the pier, said, 'No thank you.' He insisted that the public would not walk the length of the pier to see a show, however good. So, Walter Fellows and Anona Winn of Park Productions stepped in and took over. Their first show, *Star Wagon*, had the well-known radio and music-hall star, Leonard Henry, as principal comedian, and young David Lupino in support. The show did very well. 'Park Productions' also put on variety shows at the Royal Hippodrome in Eastbourne, and in 1947 Sandy was booked to work a week there. His success at this engagement led to his being booked for the following summer-season's show at the Pier.

Sandy was working at the Hackney Empire in London. Michael Lyon, the London agent, took Walter Fellows to see the show and later they went back-stage to see Sandy. 'Do you fancy a summer season at Eastbourne?' he was asked. About that time, music halls were closing all over the country, and he realised that it could be a proposition worth considering. In company with Walter Fellows he went to Eastbourne and liked what he saw. Terms and conditions were negotiated and the contract signed. When Sandy's appearance at the Pier was announced, a critic writing in a National newspaper, made the following comment: 'I understand that Sandy Powell is scheduled to star in the Pier Show at Eastbourne. Mr Powell as principal comedian is fine for Blackpool, Morecambe, Yarmouth or even Brighton, but a Yorkshire comic of his kind would be absolutely unsuitable for a high-class resort like Eastbourne.'

It was hardly the kind of notice to give an artist encouragement before he's even started a season. But, Sandy, although disappointed, decided to ignore the 'knock' and go ahead to do his best. The show was a huge success and Sandy scored a personal triumph. The local residents and holi-

153

The bill for Star Wagon *at the Pier Theatre, Eastbourne in 1948.*

daymakers took to him right away, and a delighted Walter Fellows booked him for the 1949 summer season, again to star in *Star Wagon*, but this time farther along the coast at the Pleasure Gardens, Folkestone. Fellows wanted a strong attraction at Folkestone to build up the business there, and obviously Sandy was the man to do it for him. He was right, because Sandy's success there increased box-office takings so much that Fellows wanted him to go back to Folkestone again. However, the Eastbourne Pier Company insisted that Sandy should return to Eastbourne, which he did for the summer of 1950.

At this time a young man called Norman Meadows came on the scene, who was later to become a great friend and business partner to Sandy. The introduction took place in Walter Fellows's office in Park Lane, London. Norman had just been engaged as manager for *Star Wagon* at Eastbourne. During rehearsals, Fellows told Sandy, 'Norman is quite a good performer. I'm sure that you will find him very useful in the sketches and also as a straight man.' This turned out to be true, and Norman became what Sandy described as 'one of the finest all-round performers and "feeds" I ever had.'

Apart from one summer season in Bexhill, Sussex, Sandy was principal comedian in *Star Wagon* on the Pier at Eastbourne until 1956, a six-year run that shows the esteem in which he was held by the audiences there.

Walter Fellows died the following year, and the Eastbourne Pier Company asked Sandy to put on his own show. He got together with Norman Meadows and they formed Southbourne Productions Ltd., for the purpose of presenting their own shows. *Starlight* was the name they chose for their show, which ran most successfully for fifteen summers. They mounted an entirely new production each year, and each season there were four changes of programme. Each programme was a complete revue in itself, none of the material was repeated until years later, and then only by 'special request'. It was a very ambitious scheme and it was a big challenge for them to find, plan and form new ideas and material.

The cast was selected very carefully; Sandy wanted versatile artists, who who were also pleasant people so that the season would be a happy one. To support him in the comedy line, he had Bob Andrews, a well-known radio personality, an excellent teller of stories in many dialects and an experienced compere. Others in the cast included: Horace Mashford, well-known on radio and pantomime; singing stars Clive Stock and Gwen Overton who played leading parts in *Oklahoma* and *Brigadoon*; ventriloquist Harry Benet; another fine speciality act, multi-instrumentalists Charles and Jupp; dancer Gay Owen; singer and dancer Bridie Devon; eight 'Starlights', a line of pretty chorus girls, each member of which would help in the sketches; and Kay White, Sandy's wife, a delightful character-actress and brilliant pianist, whose charming personality was an important factor in blending this talented band of players into warm, friendly, and well-balanced entertainment. There were twenty-two different scenes in this show, eleven in each half. The action was fast-moving with something to suit every taste.

The shows proved to be a greater success than ever before, and the Pier Company were highly delighted. Alf Lake, the pier secretary and manager, said, 'It was a pleasure to do business with Sandy, after that first contract was signed with him. From then on the only reason a contract was signed was to have something to show to the auditors. Sandy's word was his bond.' It was Alf Lake (who had worked on the Pier since he was a young boy), who calculated that on the 20th July 1957, Sandy would chalk up his thousandth performance on the Pier. 'This ought to be celebrated, Sandy,' he said. 'Why not put on something special, get a big star to make an appearance. You've got a month to do it, so get going.' A couple of mornings later Sandy caught the train to London and went to see impresario Billy Marsh, who handled some of the biggest stars in the world. While he was asking Billy about the possibility of someone for his gala performance, the famous film, stage, television and radio star Norman Wisdom walked in. He was handled by Billy Marsh, who remarked, 'I suppose he'd do, wouldn't he Sandy?' When Sandy explained his idea to Norman, not very hopefully, he was amazed to get the immediate reply, 'Delighted if it can possibly be arranged. Let me know the date and I'll do my damndest to fit it in somehow.' He explained, 'I want to do it because you were very helpful to me when I was looking for a break into show business. I don't know if you remember this, Sandy, but I ran into you in Charing Cross Road, and told you all my dreams and ambitions, and although you were a star and didn't know me from Adam, you took the time and trouble to give me your advice and help, and that's something I've never forgotten. This gives me a chance to repay the kindness you showed to me.' Norman was shooting the film, *Just My Luck* at Pinewood Studios and he organised things so that he could do Sandy's special show. In addition, he arranged, at his own expense, for his film and television straight man, Eddie Leslie, to work with him in the show, and brought Eddie down by air from Blackpool specially for the purpose.

The show was on a Saturday night, and the 'Saturday regulars' were Sandy's most loyal supporters. The first announcement of the appearance of Norman Wisdom was made to them a couple of weeks before the actual date of the gala performance. They were told that despite the great 'added attraction', prices would be 'as usual', and that they would be wise to get their tickets at the box-office the following Monday morning. As soon as the announcement was made public, the box-office was besieged and the house was sold out in no time. Sandy asked Billy Marsh whether Norman would prefer his arrival to be kept quiet, or whether Sandy might arrange a public welcome for him, which of course would add to the publicity and excitement. Norman sent word through that anything most helpful to Sandy would do for him. It was announced that Norman Wisdom would be at the entrance to the Pier at eleven o'clock on the Saturday morning. A tremendous crowd turned out to greet him – the streets around were packed.

Norman was marvellous. He dressed in his short, tight-fitting comedy suit, and fooled around, being photographed with anyone who wished it,

Eastbourne's favourite comedian in Starlight!

signing autographs left, right and centre. His tireless, good-humoured antics and obviously sincere friendliness were greatly appreciated by the crowds – he was a sensation. Nothing was too much trouble for him, and later, when he moved around the town, he had the place in an uproar. He did over threequarters of an hour on stage; the audience wouldn't let him go until he had given them encore after encore. After the show, he and Sandy came out of the theatre together to find that it was pouring with rain. They ran down the pier to the Ballroom, near the pier entrance, where they took shelter for a few moments. Norman asked, 'Has this ballroom got anything to do with you Sandy?'

'Not really,' replied Sandy, 'I've got a few shares in the Pier Company but that's the limit of my interest in this place.'

'Let's go in,' said Norman, and when they did, they were soon recognised. Sandy introduced Norman to the big crowd of dancers, and, despite having worked all day, Norman, after a quick consultation with the band leader, sang three songs.

The Pier Dance Band was led by Ronnie Hancox, and his vocalist was a young girl called Susan Maugham. She also took part in a show that Sandy put on every Sunday, a concert he called *Sunday Serenade*. In later years Susan Maugham found fame on stage, radio and television. It was in one of these shows that compere Bob Andrews introduced Sandy in a different manner. Instead of his usual: 'Give a warm welcome to Mr Sandy Powell.' He said, 'Here is Mr Eastbourne himself, Sandy Powell.' The title 'Mr Eastbourne', born accidentally that night, stuck, and to this day it is how Sandy is known in the town by residents and visitors alike.

For the next few years they continued with the same policy, but Norman Meadows took a more active part on stage, assisting Sandy in the sketches and becoming his straight man. Individual artists were changed almost every year, and the show was always kept fresh and up to date, so that even the visitors who came to Eastbourne every year had something new and exciting to look at.

Ever-willing to help in charity work, Sandy and his artists were constantly opening bazaars and fêtes. Eastbourne's Carnival Day with it's traditional procession through the town and great collections for charity was offered an attraction which they gladly accepted – a *Starlight* float on which Sandy and his company regaled the crowds with songs and fun. It was made up of wooden boards taken from the sides of the Pier (with full cooperation of the management) built up and decorated by the stage staff and members of the company, and set up on a large flat motor vehicle. An upright stage piano was borrowed and used for the occasion, and the pianist of the theatre band thumped out the music to lead the singing. The Starlight Girls, dressed in their stage costumes, danced and cavorted around, and their collecting boxes were always the best-filled.

Pier manager – Alf Lake – remembers incidents that occurred during the run of *Starlight* that Sandy knew nothing about at the time; just as well, because they would have upset him and put him off his work. He would

1 September each year at Eastbourne was Birthday Night for Sandy's mother.

An Evening of Olde Time Music Hall *at the Theatre Royal, Newcastle-upon-Tyne in 1964.*

have had 'pups' if he had known that one night a lady in the audience, of about eighteen stone in weight, died a few moments before the curtain was due to go up. She was sitting in the front stalls, fell forward and died. Being so heavy she was wedged in her seat and it was quite a job to release her and get her out of the theatre. It was close to curtain-up-time, so Alf sent a message backstage to delay the opening. Sandy who was, and still is, a stickler for the curtain going up bang on time, sent back frantic messages, 'What's happening, what's holding the curtain?' Alf dared not tell him; as he said, 'Sandy's so sensitive about other peoples illness's and death, he wouldn't have been able to go on that night.' Eventually the tabs went up ten minutes late, and Sandy never learned the truth of it until some time later.

On another occasion, a man and his wife reached the entrance to the theatre when the woman collapsed. It was a cold night early in the season, and Alf Lake was called to handle the situation. He quickly got into action and had one of his staff get a wheel-chair and push the unfortunate lady into a nearby dressing room. A hastily-summoned doctor pronounced her dead, which caused the elderly wardrobe-mistress to have hysterics, and upset the chorus girls in the next room. Fortunately, Sandy's dressing room was on the opposite side of the building, and he didn't know what was going on. Alf kept his fingers crossed that Sandy shouldn't find out before the ambulance came to take away the body. Just after the show had got under way, the husband, now widower, approached Alf and said, 'What about our tickets, it wasn't my fault that they weren't used. They cost me seven bob, can I have my money back?' This, apart from his amazement at the request, put him in a bit of a quandary because of the strict rule that 'money cannot be refunded if tickets are not used on the night of performance.' The usual practice was to offer seats for another night, but in this case, he could hardly do so!

The *Daily Express* used to stage a 'Round Britain Air Race', with the finishing point a few miles along the coast at Brighton. Different types of aircraft entered and were handicapped accordingly. The handicappers' aim was to get a thrilling finish, and on this last run-in to the finishing point, groups of planes were roaring past the theatre. This thrilling and spectacular sight drew thousands of spectators to the sea-front, and particularly on to the pier – including a full-house audience booked to see the show. However good a show might be, it couldn't compete against this sort of thing and the curtain was held until all the planes had gone by. The performance started twenty minutes after advertised time. It was the one and only occasion that Sandy didn't complain since he and his company had thoroughly enjoyed the wonderful spectacle.

On another occasion the battleship *Vanguard* paid Eastbourne a courtesy visit and was anchored some way off the pier. The *Starlight* company was invited to take tea with the ship's officers and a pinnace was sent to take them aboard. They were provided with a fine spread but something went wrong with the arrangements to get them back to the pier. At departure time it was found that the pinnace was not available and the company was put into one of the ship's boats for the return journey. It was low water, the boat hit a sandbank and they stuck fast, stranded close to the pier. They could see the audience streaming in to the theatre, little knowing that the entire company and stage staff were out at sea. The curtain rang up twenty minutes late, which, under the circumstances, wasn't too bad.

A charity which Sandy supported was the National Society for Cancer Relief. In response to a special appeal for an extra effort to raise badly needed funds, Sandy went once again to Billy Marsh in London, and asked whether any of his star clients would be helpful. 'I suppose you might consider Frankie Vaughan, if I can manage to get him?' said Billy. 'You bet I would,' replied Sandy, and to his great delight, a couple of days later, Billy Marsh rang through to say that Frankie would be happy to do the show in question. However, the issue was complicated by the fact that, on the night in question, Frankie was booked to appear in the TV show *Sunday Night At The London Palladium*, but insisted that it was changed to another date in order to accommodate Sandy. A gesture that was really a measure of the respect that Sandy was held in by his follow artists. Sandy was so delighted about Frankie doing the show that a couple of days before the night, he rang Billy Marsh. 'Please tell Frankie that I've arranged that any number of rooms he wants will be at his disposal at the Queens Hotel. A table has been booked for him and as many friends as he wants to invite. Everything is laid on, wines, cigars, the lot. It's all on my personal account, not a farthing will come out of the takings.'

Billy commented, 'That will cost you a pretty penny, Sandy.'

'No matter, I'm thrilled that Frankie is coming down here for me, and I'm very happy that the expenses will be on me.'

Billy telephoned later to say, 'Frankie asked me to say thank you to you but he'd rather have two bottles of beer and some sandwiches in the dressing-room, and nothing else!'

Sandy knew that Frankie used a microphone to great effect, and he wanted to make sure that nothing would go wrong in this respect. The mikes at the theatre were good, but to be safe he asked his stage manager to lay on a spare, and, to make doubly certain there would be no slip-up, to get in touch with Frankie's office to ensure they brought one with them. Frankie made another marvellous gesture, he brought along his own accompanying group, 'The V Men', entirely at his own expense.

The theatre was packed from floor to ceiling, and Frankie's first number was received rapturously. During the second item the microphone dropped on the floor and was put out of action. Sandy thought, 'Thank goodness we have a spare laid on', but that was found to be defective. Frankie, spotting Sandy standing out front, called out to him 'That's show business, but don't worry, we've got one of ours.' Incredibly, that didn't work either. Three microphones and none worked. Frank apologised to the audience, but a man called out: 'You don't need one of those things, Frankie, sing without it.' 'Okay,' replied Frankie, 'I'll cut out the beat numbers and sing you some ballads.' And that is what he did for the next forty-five minutes, getting an ovation that he said he would never forget. The show raised over fifteen hundred pounds for the Cancer Fund.

The first night every September was a 'Special Gala Night' given over to the celebration of the birthday of Sandy's Mother. She was brought on during the finale to receive birthday greetings and tributes from the company, staff and regulars among the faithful patrons. It was a demonstration of affection for the woman who had worked so hard and sacrificed so much to bring her son to stardom. Sandy had by that time played female characters in sketches and pantomime, and on this gala occasion used to wear a dress similar to the one worn by his mother and a silver wig, so when he introduced her to the audience they looked like sisters. This delightful little ceremony went on until Lily died in 1963.

Because of his mother's illness, Sandy wanted to give the 1963 season a miss, but the Pier Company persuaded him to stay. The Eastbourne Corporation had taken over the huge and beautiful Congress Theatre which had been specially built for them and would provide stiff opposition to the Pier Theatre. In these circumstances they didn't want to take a chance of having a show without Sandy, who was a tremendous draw with holiday-makers and residents. Sandy agreed to stay on, and, despite the opposition of an all-star show in a beautiful new theatre, *Starlight* more than held its own and increased its takings at the box-office. Sandy was persuaded to stay on for another season to confirm that the Pier Theatre could meet all opposition if the show was good, and that Eastbourne could support two summer shows. He did this on the understanding that he would reorganise the show to allow him to take things a little easier.

So, having completed fifteen very happy and successful seasons at the Pier Theatre, Sandy announced that *Starlight* of 1965 would have Ken Roberts as principal comedian, supported by a large and talented cast, produced by Sandy Powell and Norman Meadows. Norman became responsible for the management of the show, and also supported Ken Roberts in the sketches. As his straight man, and combining magic and fun, they had a clever young man called John Wade (now a star in his own field) and the rest of the carefully chosen cast consisted of vocalists, specialities, and a line of pretty young ladies directed by a famous choreographer. The show was moulded into a first-class summer entertainment, one of the most popular and successful in the country.

Although in his sixty-fifth year, a time when most men retire, and despite his intention to take things easier, Sandy, after seeing the Eastbourne show safely and successfully off the ground, went off to work as 'Star Guest Artist' for many summer weeks at The Pavilion Llandudno in North Wales. His friend, the famous rubber-necked comedian Nat Jackley was the resident comedian.

Ken Roberts was a great success at Eastbourne, so Sandy put him in again the following year, with Norman Meadows, Betty Emery, Jock Morgan, Roy Earl, and the popular singers Gwen Overton and Clive Stock. It proved to be another winner. Sandy worked a very hectic summer season in Worthing, with the famous *Fol de Rols*, a show he had always greatly admired, he was the 'Star Guest Artist' doing two spots from his music-hall repertoire. A young artist in the show whom he greatly admired was a comedian called Don Smoothey, and he noted him for 'future reference' for *Starlight* in Eastbourne.

Starlight 1967 brought Ken Roberts for the third successive year but, apart from Norman Meadows (working better than ever), the rest of the cast were mainly new to Eastbourne. After rehearsing and seeing *Starlight* 1967 safely away, Sandy went off to work the season at the Spa Pavilion, on the East coast in the Edward Kent production of *The Sandy Powell Show*. He returned to Eastbourne to appear in *Sunday Starlight* every week, as 'Guest Artist' – so much for his decision to 'take things easier'!

For *Starlight* 1968 Sandy brought in the young man with whom he had been so impressed in the *Fol's* – Don Smoothey, as principal comedian, with

The Pier Theatre at Eastbourne on fire . . .

164

. . . while Sandy and Kay look on, helpless.

a clever conjurer-comedian Frankie Holmes as speciality and second comic.
He also employed a fine male singer, Tommy Wright, who, showing aptitude for playing comedy, was soon whisked into the sketches and later
became very successful in television plays. Sandy's summer stint in his
sixty-eighth year was a strenuous season of one-night stands as 'Guest
Star' in an *Old Tyme Music Hall Show* playing Clacton, Essex, on the East
Coast on Monday nights, Folkestone, Kent on Wednesdays, Weston Super
Mare, Somerset, on Thursdays, and then on Sunday nights at various
theatres in different parts of the country. Sandy says that although this
was 'most enjoyable', it did mean a 'terrific lot of driving,' – an understate-
ment!

Don Smoothey was a great success in Eastbourne, but Sandy couldn't
book him for the 1969 *Starlight* show because of a prior engagement. He
took a chance and promoted Frankie Holmes to principal comic. Although
he had been a big success as second comic to Don, he lacked that extra
experience: Sandy, however, was confident that Frankie could rise to the
occasion, which he did, and, after seeing a successful opening, he set off on
another of his summer seasons in 'old-tyme' music hall. This time, however, it was a resident show. He had been offered another run round of one-
night, stands, but politely refused – once was enough! The show was an Ed.
W. Jones production, *Let's All Go To The Music Hall*, at the Knightstone
Pavilion Theatre in Weston Super Mare, with an excellent chairman and
master of ceremonies, Eddie Reindeer, the queen of music-hall singers,
the beautiful and statuesque, Margery Manners, Peter Cavanagh, the great
radio and music-hall favourite with his uncanny voice impressions of
popular stars, and the famous 'Strolling Vagabond' of song – Cavan
O'Connor.

Sandy at this time was working harder than ever; he loved the summer-
revue type of entertainment which meant working in front of people with
whom he had a great rapport.

In 1970, Trust Houses Ltd., the big hotel and catering group, took over
the Pier Company. Sandy saw one of their directors and said, 'I suppose
that you will be wanting to make a change in future?'

'Certainly not,' was the reply, 'we'd like you to carry on. You have been
doing wonderful business and that suits us fine. We won't interfere in any
way. But, for our opening season, may I suggest that you put in a big
television star.'

'That would cost a lot of money,' commented Sandy. 'Ours is a family
show, with a well-balanced cast and good production, run on a reasonably
modest budget, and it's proved very successful with our type of audience.'

The director replied, 'Don't worry about the money for star names, we
will look after that side. We would like to make a splash for the start, so go
after somebody like Tom Jones or Englebert Humperdinck, stars of that
calibre.'

Sandy tried, but found, as he had expected, that their asking-fee was
astronomical, the sort of money only big-capacity theatres could pay. A

compromise was made by booking one of the big radio names of the day, singer Ronnie Hilton, the brilliant impressionist Margo Henderson, and comedian Billy Burdon Jnr – three strong solid performers as the supporting 'names'. Sandy and his partner Norman Meadows, having the contracts of these artists signed, sat back confident that their show, scheduled to start in the middle of May, would bring them another triumphantly successful summer season.

Alas, it was not to be. On the Thursday afternoon of 8th January, 1970, fire destroyed the Eastbourne Pier Theatre. Huge flames, fanned by strong winds, gutted the main stage and dressing-rooms area. Thousands of pounds worth of valuable theatrical scenery, wardrobe, curtains and props were lost. It was the biggest fire disaster in Eastbourne for many years. Crowds of shoppers and residents poured on to the sea-front to watch the Eastbourne Fire Brigade and a half-dozen supporting units from all over Sussex, combine in an effort to save the doomed theatre. Over sixty firemen, many wearing breathing apparatus, gallantly tackled the task of saving what they could of the theatre, and of the pier itself. Because the safety-curtain was down when the fire broke out, it contained the fire to the back stage. This gave the firemen a chance to get their hoses working effectively inside the auditorium, and, by the time the safety-curtain finally collapsed, they had things well under control. It was a bitterly cold day, and about an hour after the fire started, showers of hail were blown on to the pier by a high wind. The hail later turned to snow, and it was in these dreadful conditions that the magnificent work of the firemen and pier staff saved the pier.

Sandy and his wife Kay were at home just a couple of hundred yards away. Hearing the sound of the sirens near by, they walked towards the pier, and turning the corner of their road, they saw a huge crowd of people, lots of fire engines and police busily controlling the movement of traffic and people. They managed to get on to the pier and had to stand helplessly by, watching the firemen pour thousands of gallons of water through the windows of the dressing-rooms and stores, destroying their scenery, costumes and props. It was a heartbreaking sight. Sandy said to Kay, 'What on earth are we going to do, here I am, seventy years old, what is going to happen – this is the end.' Norman Meadows was staying with a friend in Camberley, Surrey, where Sandy telephoned him, 'Have you heard that our lovely theatre is on fire?'

Norman enquired, 'Is it bad?'

'Bad,' replied Sandy, 'it's all gone, everything.' Norman drove immediately to Eastbourne and was shocked when he saw the smouldering remains of the theatre.

The next morning the partners walked around the wreckage and realised that there was much to discuss about the future. First, they tried to get the show booked into another venue. It was no use because the dates at which a company of that calibre could be booked had long since been snapped up. Contractually, the artists' engagements, for the run of the show, were null and void. The position was as bad for them as it was for Sandy and Norman. The fire had thrown them all out of work, but Southbourne Productions (Sandy and Norman) in addition suffered the loss of scenery, costumes and properties.

In the friendliest manner, the partnership was dissolved since Norman had received a good offer from Trust Houses to carry on at the pier in a managerial capacity, and Sandy carried on working his act, with his wife Kay. New Scotland Yard was called in to investigate the cause of the fire, and their findings led eventually to the arrest of a man on a charge of arson.

Actually it was his second attempt to start a fire. On the previous Monday, Sandy and Norman had had their usual weekly meeting with Alf Lake in his office. At its conclusion they walked along the pier and smelt something burning. The fire brigade was called and the source of the smell located under the stage, a minor fire of some sacking catching alight. It didn't look deliberate and when dealt with was promptly forgotten. The arsonist seeing his first attempt fail, tried again. This time he succeeded with the consequent disastrous effect.

After he was arrested he confessed his responsibility for the crime. When the judge asked him why he had deliberately set fire to the pier, he replied that he had quarrelled with his wife and wanted to do something to annoy her! He was confined to Broadmoor Criminal Asylum.

10

A Golden Year

WATCHING their theatre go up in smoke and flame was a traumatic experience for Kay and Sandy. 'That's the end,' said Sandy, 'I'm seventy, what can I do, this is the finale.'

But a 'good fairy somewhere up there' must have waved a magic wand. It surely had to be something like that because what followed could have only come out of the pages of a book of fairy tales.

The very next day an old friend Bunny Baron telephoned Sandy and after commiserating with him over his atrocious luck asked, 'Sandy, how many summer seasons have you had on the pier?'

'Twenty,' was the reply.

'I've had an idea. Instead of you doing one-night stands for me in the summer as arranged, why don't you make it twenty-one years at Eastbourne?'

'But I haven't got a theatre,' protested Sandy.

'I know you haven't,' said Bunny, 'but Arthur has, why don't you go into his *Golden Years*. Give it some thought.' A few minutes after putting down the receiver, the telephone rang again, it was Arthur Lane.

'Sandy, I've been thinking. What about you coming into *The Golden Years* at the Hippodrome this summer and celebrating your twenty-first year in Eastbourne as my Star Guest Artist.' This apparent coincidence was of course, a well-arranged plan by two kind and thoughtful friends. Arthur and Bunny, in the years before they had become famous impresarios, had been through the hoop as performers and knew the ups and downs of the business. They stepped in just at the right time to give Sandy a 'lift' when it was most needed. Although the fire was disastrous, it didn't leave Sandy in any financial difficulty. The great blow was to his love of performing and the pleasure he could give to audiences.

He was very happy to sign on with Arthur. The previous year, *The Golden Years* at the Royal Hippodrome had been in opposition to *Starlight*, at the pier. Both shows had done well. Arthur Lane and his partner Audrey Lupton were directing the Wimbledon Theatre, in Surrey. At that time they had on Harold Fielding's production *Half-a-Sixpence* starring Tommy Steele for a two-week run-in before opening in the West End at the Cambridge Theatre. Fielding asked Arthur to release him on the last Saturday

169

night so that he could get the show taken down at Wimbledon and set up again at the Cambridge in time on the following Tuesday for a special charity performance under Royal patronage. He promised proper financial recompense for the loss of Arthur's Saturday-night house. Arthur agreed, but was left with the problem of having his theatre 'dark' on a night when business was good and also of disappointing his Saturday-night regulars. He had a brainwave. 'Audrey,' he said, 'let's do an old-tyme-music-hall night. We'll use our own repertory people and I'll try and get Randolph Sutton to top the bill.' This was quickly organised, and 'slips' were pasted across the bills outside the theatre announcing that the Saturday night performance was cancelled and replaced by an all-star old-tyme music-hall show headed by Randolph Sutton. The next day Kay and Sandy called at the theatre to pick up some costumes they had lent Arthur and Audrey. Seeing the notice Sandy remarked, 'That looks good, Arthur, we'll come in to see that.'

'You'll do nothing of the sort, I'm not letting you in to see it.'

Puzzled, Sandy asked, 'What's up? Have we got leprosy or something, why can't we see it?'

Arthur replied, 'Because you'll be in it, so what about it Sandy?' It was an impromptu thought by Arthur, and Sandy agreed, equally quickly. The arrangement was made that Sandy would be announced as the 'Surprise Guest Artist'. On the Saturday morning Arthur, wondering how bookings were going, not expecting much because of the short notice about the substitute show, was amazed to be told that the box-office had been besieged the moment the notice went up and that the house was completely sold out!

Sandy says that the audience that night was marvellous, the atmosphere was electric, and that he had never before played to such a responsive audience. Impresario Don Ross then invited Sandy to appear in his long-running show *Thanks for the Memory* with all-time greats Gertie Gitana, G. H. Elliott, Nellie Wallace, Ella Shields and Talbot O'Farrell. Don Ross, a music hall performer and husband of Gertie Gitana, was a highly respected agent who produced and toured many variety and circus shows. Sandy thinks that Don Ross, Arthur Lane and Don Ellis (for whom he worked many times in pantomime and variety) have each a marvellous knowledge of music hall. Arthur, delighted and inspired, decided to form his own company of 'old stars' and had no difficulty in persuading Sandy to join in the show which he called *Nights at the Tivoli*. It enjoyed a most successful tour of Moss and Stoll dates. Sandy and Arthur became friends, and it was no wonder that when Sandy was shattered by the disastrous fire on the pier at Eastbourne, that Arthur Lane was one of the first to put out a helping hand.

Another surprise came to Sandy soon after he had signed the summer-season contract. J. Huckerby, a director of Bass Charrington, the famous Brewery group, wrote: 'Miss Hetty King has advised me to write you about a new public house we are opening just outside the City Centre of Rotherham, Yorkshire, and we have been seeking through Rotherham's past

*The Sandy Powell Lounge at The Comedian. And seated with Sandy are
J. Huckerby (left) and G. V. Parker.*

history for a name for the house. It came to our knowledge that you were born in Rotherham and have close association with the city. We wondered if you would be agreeable for the new public house to be named after you, or have some association, with your goodself. Please let me know whether the idea interests you, as in choosing a public-house name we have, of course, to bear in mind the interior decor, which has a great bearing on the end result. Yours sincerely, . . .' Sandy was thrilled and flattered, because this would be the very first time that a public house would bear the name of a living music-hall performer. But his innate modesty got the better of his common-sense, and he declined the suggestion that the house should be named after him personally, but instead he proposed that the name should be 'The Comedian'. The company agreed, but insisted that they would like the saloon bar to be called the 'Sandy Powell Lounge', with the appropriate music-hall decor. To this Sandy assented, as did he also to their invitation to perform the opening ceremony by 'pulling the first pint'.

Sandy's opening at the Royal Hippodrome in *The Golden Years of Music Hall*, his twenty-first summer season in Eastbourne, brought loads of telegrams from friends and admirers. One that pleased him especially read 'Congratulations on celebration your 21st Trust you are getting the Keys of Eastbourne greetings David Frost.' Then followed a wonderful season and, during the run, rumours floated around that there was a possibility of the show being taken over to South Africa. As the weeks went by with nothing more being said about it, Sandy put it out of his mind. On the last night of the show Arthur saw Sandy backstage and said that Sam Peltz, managing director of 'Capitol Entertainments of South Africa', was out front watching the show and was wanting to meet Sandy and talk about going to South Africa. Over a drink later in Sandy's dressing-room, Mr Peltz said that he had fixed to take the show over there and that he would like Sandy in the show. 'Certainly,' said Sandy, and that made another delightful happening in a year that had started so disastrously. But, as if that wasn't enough, more good news was on its way.

Betty Jacoby, Sandy's agent, telephoned to say that Leslie Grade wanted him for a show on the 12th November. Sandy replied, 'You know I've booked to see the Royal Performance. Tell him I'm sorry, but I won't miss seeing that show.'

Betty replied, 'I told him that, but he said that you will have to miss seeing it that night, because you will be appearing in the show!' And so Sandy was booked to appear in his third Royal Performance, and in addition, the Grade organisation wanted him for six weeks at the London Palladium.

Jimmy Green, eminent theatrical columnist of the *Evening News*, commenting about the Royal Show, headed his page with a bold line reading: 'Sandy Powell asks "Can You Hear Me Queen Mother?" ' That year, H.M. Queen Mother was patron of the Royal Variety Performance, and a couple of weeks before the show, Elsie and Doris Waters (of 'Gert and Daisy' fame) told Sandy that they had helped Her Royal Highness at a charity function and mentioned that one of their friends, Sandy Powell, was appearing in the forthcoming show. She had replied, 'Isn't he the man that says "Can you hear me Mother?"' Sandy was thrilled to hear that the Queen Mother had remembered his catch-phrase over thirty years after he had spoken it on the air. He was also immensely pleased that during the after-show presentation, she made a point of speaking to Sandy and Kay, saying,

Bernard Delfont presents Kay and Sandy to the Queen Mother at the Royal Performance in 1970. On Sandy's right is Caterina Valente.

An after-show celebration. Standing on Max Bygraves's left are Peggy, Sandy's daughter, and her husband Brian. Seated are Ida on the left and Kay on the right.

'I was with our mutual friends Gert and Daisy. They do think highly of you both. I understand that Mrs Powell was on the stage before you were married.' Bernard Delfont commented, 'Yes, ma'am, Mrs Powell was one of Mr Cochran's young ladies and played in many of his shows at the London Pavilion, which I am sure you must have seen.' And indeed she had, and chatted with Kay about them, for Her Royal Highness had been a great theatre-goer.

Sandy's ventriloquist's act is considered a music-hall burlesque of the highest class. Like so many of his gems it started out as a gag in one of his road shows. In response to Sandy's request for a good broad comedy act for the *Road Show*, his agent booked him a ventriloquist. He turned out to be a disaster and his act usually received a minimum of applause, leaving a dead spot for the following artist to fill. To liven things up Sandy hastily put together a few gags with a vent dummy, a two-minute spot of outrageous comedy. Realising that again it was an idea that could be built up, he kept on adding bits here and there, and it eventually became a fifteen-minute routine which, together with 'The Magician' became classics of burlesque comedy.

Many famous magicians were numbered among Sandy's fans, and this was shown when The International Brotherhood of Magicians invited him to appear in a gala show at their convention in Eastbourne. He was understandably nervous at being on the same bill with world-famous professional magicians and doing an act which was a send-up of their own line of business to an audience of over twelve-hundred magicians. They obviously enjoyed his beautifully observed over-played manipulations of a self-important prestidigator, for they gave him a great ovation and he took many curtain calls.

Another 'Golden Moment' came when the BBC asked him to appear in a play called *Don't Ring Us, We'll Ring You*, in which he played the part of the secretary of a Working Men's Club. TV personality John Junkin played a supporting role, and it was a most successful and enjoyable experience.

Next followed what was one of the most extraordinary happenings of all during this year. Kay and Sandy were in Betty Jacoby's office talking of how thrilled they were at being selected to appear in the Royal Performance, and the kindness of Jimmy Green giving Sandy such a wonderful 'plug' in the *Evening News*. As they were leaving, Kay leant across Betty's desk to give her a good-bye kiss, and she felt something being pressed surreptitiously into her hand. Obviously it was meant for her alone, so she waited until an opportunity arose for her to see what it was all about. On a piece of paper was written the message, 'Please ring me.' A few moments before leaving Betty's office an artist had come in to see her and Kay thought that the secrecy was because of this, and that the message was for Sandy, something that Betty could not speak of in the presence of the other artist. Making their way to Sheekeys the sea-food restaurant very popular with show-business people, Kay told Sandy about Betty's note, and while they were there he telephoned Betty, who told him that it wasn't anything special. Sandy, very puzzled, said to Kay: 'I don't know what that was all about, she just told me things we'd already spoken about, she must be getting forgetful.' It then crossed Kay's mind that the message was intended for her, and not Sandy. She thought, 'Oh dear, something's gone wrong about the Royal Show and Betty wants me to break the news gently to Sandy.' At Sheekeys, there was a public telephone downstairs, next to the ladies' room. This provided an excuse for Kay to telephone Betty.

'Why did you get Sandy to 'phone me, I wanted to talk to you about something we've got to keep very secret. Thames TV want to do a *This Is Your Life* programme on Sandy, and they want your cooperation.'

Kay said, 'How marvellous! Of course, I'll help.' Little did she know what she had let herself in for. White lies had to concocted to keep it all from Sandy, life became difficult and very complicated. It was exciting but very nerve-wracking.

Kay knew very little about Sandy's early life, the years before she had met him. There was only two people who knew about his personal life and those were his daughter, Peggy and son, Peter. Jack Crawshaw was in charge

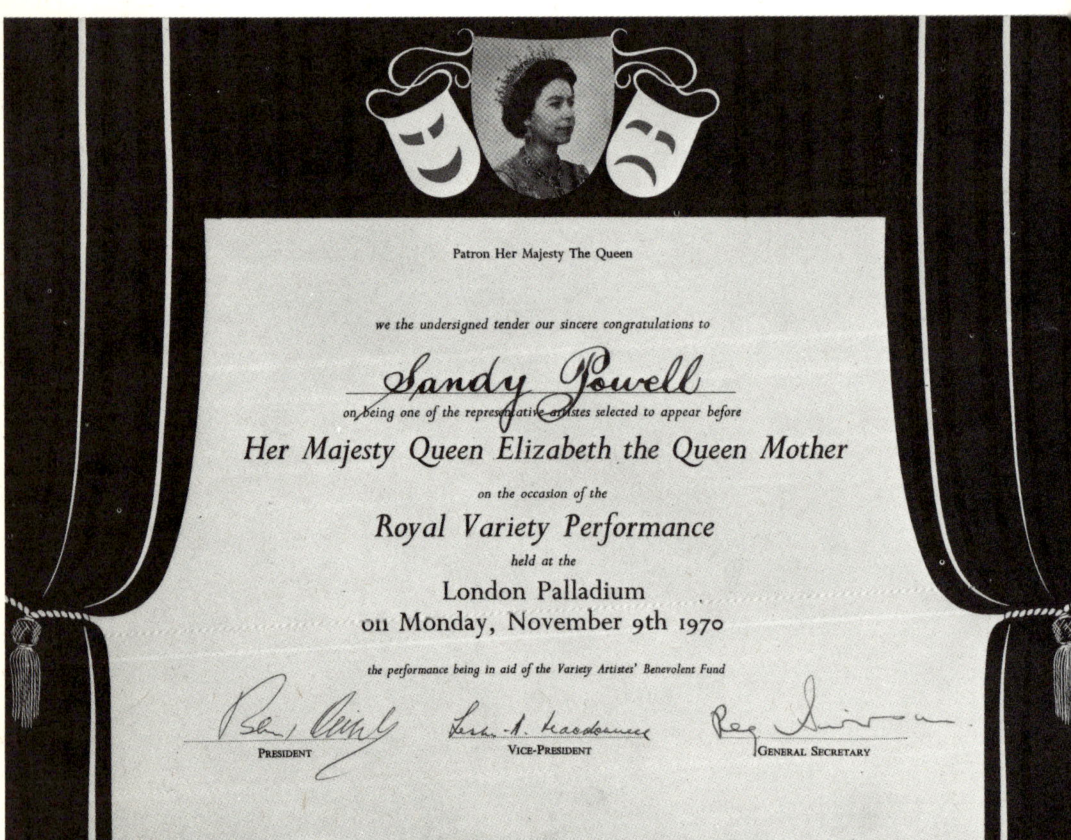

The congratulation certificate for the 1970 Royal Performance.

of operations at Thames TV, and it was a devious business establishing contact without Sandy knowing. That was the first problem to be solved. Obviously a regular line of communication had to be set up. The telephone at home could not be used because she and Sandy were always together. Kay then remembered their friend Norman Meadows who was now manager of the pier, just around the corner. He was a constant and regular caller at the house and therefore a perfect message-carrier and contact man. Thames could telephone him and their message could be conveyed to Kay during his regular, almost daily visits to their house. Norman remembers, with amusement how Kay first approached him about the matter. Through his secretary she sent a message that she wanted to see him urgently, and in private.

When she first came to his office her manner was almost furtive and he wondered whether there was some serious personal trouble. This was soon dispelled when she said 'Norman, Thames want to have Sandy on *This Is Your Life*, and we have to get a place where we can have messages taken and organised generally. Can it be done here?' Norman, thrilled by the honour being paid to his great friend, readily gave his assent and promise of full cooperation. Pier director Alf Lake agreed to his office being used as the 'secret operations centre'. Jack Crawshaw was notified immediately, Kay put him in the picture, explaining her difficulties, which could only be solved by getting the help of their friend and partner Norman Meadows to set up lines of communication between herself and London. She also mentioned Peggy as the only means of finding out about Sandy's early life, and Bert Montague, the first man that gave him a big break. She wanted his permission to approach them. 'That would be great,' he said, 'but, please do emphasise the necessity for absolute secrecy. Not the slightest hint must be given to anyone.'

Clandestine telephone calls to Peggy and Bert Montague were made and their participation was sought and delightedly agreed to, and the snowball started to roll. A tricky preliminary was the problem of excuses for Kay to get out of the house on her own, without rousing suspicion. Kay had to use all her natural feminine intuition to make up a battery of excuses, and she knew that she couldn't overdo it. Norman who normally dropped in for 'elevenses' gave Kay the 'wink' when she was needed to go to the office to do a bit of phoning. As time went by things became more devious and complicated; Kay was almost running out of excuses. How it was all done without Sandy finding out, will for ever remain a mystery as far as Kay is concerned. So much had to be done, gathering up programmes, photographs and posters for Thames to enlarge for projection on to the big screen in the TV studio. Tracing the people connected with Sandy's past, his helpers and colleagues was a mammoth task. In this respect the Thames research team worked wonders. Nothing was too much trouble for them. Kay would say, 'I know there was a young boy named Jimmy Fletcher who sang in Sandy's *Road Show* in the thirties. I believe he lived somewhere near Sheffield.'

'Leave that to us,' they replied, and trace him they did, much to Sandy's delight when he saw him on the show eventually, after so many years. The same thing happened with Roy Jeffries, who Kay remembered had once been mentioned by Sandy, who described him as a 'great feed' and character actor he had with him in his shows and films. 'Where does he live?' Kay was asked.

'Somewhere near Coventry, I believe,' was her reply. It was as vague as that, but they found him. It is doubtful whether the millions who view this popular programme have any idea of the enormous amount of work that goes into its preparation. The skill and patience of the organising and research staff is almost limitless.

The final problem was the toughest of all to solve – the pretext to get him to the studio without arousing his suspicion. Arthur Lane came up with a brilliant idea. He told Thames that Sandy was going to South Africa with his *Golden Years* show. 'I can tell Sandy that I have been requested by the management there to make a short filmed interview and an excerpt of one of Sandy's routines for them to use as a trailer-advertisement to publicise the forthcoming tour.' Thames were thrilled with the idea and promised their utmost cooperation. Arthur told Sandy about the proposed film and said he would prepare a script for him to learn. Kay said that when Arthur gave him the script he took it all very seriously and sat up studying it thoroughly until he had got it all off 'pat'. Arthur, a first-class producer in his own right went to London to view the studio set-up to make sure that his idea was properly used. The Thames TV building in Euston Road London, was next door to the Rank building, and the name 'Rank' in neon-lights was displayed at the top of the building, so Arthur suggested that the dummy cameras used in the supposed film studio should each have the name 'Rank Films' inscribed on a plate fixed to the camera to replace the 'Thames TV' already on them. The proposed entrance to be used was to be sign-posted with the name 'Rank Films', as were all the notices and plates of the rooms in the corridor leading to the studio, which included the name of Eamon Andrews, whose office was in that particular corridor. A great deal of trouble was taken to ensure that everything that might look sus-picious was removed and replaced by things more appropriate.

Another complication arose when Kay and Norman were asked to attend the rehearsal on the day before the show. By sheer coincidence it was the day that Sandy had to go to London to do the commentary on the documen-tary film being made by the BBC about Fred Karno's disastrous venture at Taggs Island. Kay said that if it hadn't been for that, she would not have known what excuse to use to cover her journey to London. But there was another hurdle to cross in respect to Sandy's 'Karno trip'. Kay always accompanies Sandy. Wherever he goes, whatever he does, Sandy likes her by his side. There is a wonderful rapport between them. 'How on earth am I going to get out of this?' she wondered. She left it until the very morning of departure and said to Sandy, 'I will go to town with you with the greatest

Sandy (the Ventriloquist) with Eamonn Andrews on This is your life.

pleasure, but I don't know the first thing about Fred Karno and I won't be able to help you in any way.'

Sandy replied, 'That's all right, love, it's a lousy day, you'll get cold hanging around in the open at Taggs Island doing nothing. Come down on a later train, let's meet at Sheekeys this evening, say around seven, we'll have dinner and perhaps see a show.' A taxi had been ordered to get them to Eastbourne station in good time to catch the early train to London, but Sandy went off on his own. Kay hurriedly got in touch with Norman Meadows and arranged for him to pick her up at the house to catch a later

A reflective Sandy, with support from Georgie Wood, accepts the volume from Eamonn Andrews.

train together. It was only later they realised that it could have all been easily misunderstood by the neighbours!

Norman had actually been in London the previous day for a rehearsal, and had caught the last train back to Eastbourne. Kay was wanted at the final rehearsal, to see where she was to sit during the show and to run through her lines about her life with Sandy. As arranged, she met Sandy who told her what had happened that day at Taggs Island, and they had a very happy evening and stayed in London for the night. At the appointed time on the next day, 25th November 1970, Arthur Lane arrived in a chauffeur-driven car, supplied by the studio to take them to Euston Road. He brought with him a large suitcase in which were packed Sandy's working clothes and props. Also included, and unbeknown to Sandy, was a dinner jacket, shirt and shoes into which he was to quickly change immediately after being 'discovered filming', by Eamon Andrews. It had to be a very quick change as it was only a short walk to the hall where the invited studio audience was waiting to greet him. A little way off from the studio Arthur suggested that they stop at a pub for a drink before they went to the studio. 'Good idea,' said Sandy and they found a nice place. Sandy went to the bar to get the drinks and Arthur said to Kay, 'Before we leave here, make sure that Sandy goes to the men's room. If he doesn't, it will just be our luck if he wants to go when we are there, and he will bash into Eamon Andrews. Just before we leave here, I will say to Sandy: "Why not go to the men's here?" and you back me up.' This request puzzled Sandy, but he did what he was asked, but when they were walking to the car, he remarked quietly to Kay, 'Why was Arthur anxious I went to the men's before we get to the studio?'

'You know Arthur' replied Kay. 'You know how cautious he is. We are on a tight schedule, they may want you to get on with the filming as soon as we get there, it's the sensible thing to do really.' When they arrived at the entrance to the building, the notice on the door reading 'Rank Film Studio', gave Sandy no clue that things were different to what they were supposed to be. The commissionaire whispered to Kay, 'Hold it a couple of minutes, while they get Mr Andrews and his staff out of the way.' Kay responded by keeping Sandy busy until she got the all-clear sign from the doorman. As soon as they got to their dressing-room and deposited their cases, Sandy wanted to go out and have a look round. Kay had to make all sorts of excuses to persuade him to stay put. 'They might call us any minute, let us dress first and have a look round later.' They were tense nerve-wracking minutes. If Sandy had seen anything of the cast of the evening's 'main event', it would have ruined everything.

Sandy, dressed in his officer's uniform, and Kay, dressed in the clothes she wore in the act, were eventually called to the studio where the film was being shot. The technicians and lighting men went about their work as they normally would, as did the men on the cameras who measured the distances for correct focussing – all the things necessary in the way of preliminaries before the actual filming. They performed their various tasks and went through the motions so seriously that there wasn't a chance for Sandy to realise it was all false. Later when all was revealed, Sandy said, 'I wish I had those men on contract, what a bunch of actors!'

Arthur directed operations, first running through the short interview and then Sandy's act up to the point where Kay made an entrance to say accusingly to Sandy, 'I saw your lips moving.' This was the arranged cue for Eamon to enter and start the ball rolling. But nothing happened, Eamon wasn't there. Arthur thinking quickly said, 'Let us try it again.' They did, but the same thing happened, Eamon did not enter.' Let's do it just once more,' said Arthur. Sandy whispered to Kay, 'What's the matter with Arthur? I've done this sketch for over twenty-five years, doesn't he think I know the ruddy thing by now.' Realising that Sandy was getting a bit jumpy and about to ask for another repeat, Arthur caught the signal that Eamon was standing by and said, 'Let's just have it from your line, Kay,' and when she said, 'I saw your lips moving', Eamon came into sight and said, 'Sandy, I also saw your lips moving.' Before he could say another word Sandy exclaimed, 'Eamon Andrews! How nice to see you, do you realise that we have both been in the business for years yet this is the first time we've ever met.' He didn't realise what was happening until Eamon showed him the book and said 'Sandy Powell, this is your life.' Even at this moment Sandy couldn't grasp it and he was still in a daze when Kay led him away to change into a dinner jacket.

Only a couple of minutes after this shock, a packed and very enthusiastic audience greeted him on an occasion when he was to have his past life unfolded before him and millions of viewers. He was to meet once again colleagues he hadn't seen for years who had come long distances to pay tribute to him. Eamon in his own inimitable way started with the words, 'Well Sandy that sketch of yours I interrupted is one of the many you have used in your career that spans sixty-five years of success; films, records, stage, radio and television.' Eamon then introduced a succession of people who had come into his life: his dear wife Kay, then his daughter Peggy, son Peter, son-in-law Brian and his grandchildren. Also there were a young lady called Pat Pilkington who was now famous as Pat Phoenix (Elsie Tanner), star of *Coronation Street*, Bert Montague, the man who gave him his first big break, Roy Jeffries, a super 'feed', and boy soprano Jimmy Fletcher who both assisted Sandy in the 1935 Royal Show. Jessie Matthews, who also appeared on that same programme, Bert Murfin, who for over twenty years had been Sandy's stage manager and general factotum attended, as did Evelyn Laye, a great theatrical personality with whom he had often worked in many presentations. This was followed by the presence of a lady whom Sandy considers the finest artist he ever worked with, Hetty King, who at the age of eighty-six was still working. Then a star of international fame and fellow Water Rat, Frankie Vaughan, who had flown over from America especially to be on the programme said: 'Because of the great respect we have for Sandy in the business, and because he epitomises all the good things that we hope to become, a man all the comics laugh at, and all the boys in the business love, but, most of all the man we aspire to be, a man with great respect and a great pro.' This was a wonderful tribute from a fellow star to someone greatly beloved by every member of the profession. Finally, there appeared someone who was himself a national institution of show business, and who had in 1915 booked Sandy to deputize for him, when he was known as 'Wee Georgie Wood'. The memorable session ended with Eamon handing over the book and saying the magic words, 'Sandy Powell, this is your life.'

Most viewers believe that the recipient takes away this volume to cherish as a memory of a wonderful occasion. This is not so. The volume used by Eamon which viewers see on the screen is a 'dummy book', in which are written the notes and cues to guide him through the programme he handles so expertly. Around three weeks later the postman brought Sandy a parcel containing a handsome red leather-bound volume. Engraved in gold on the front cover are the words: 'This is Your Life Sandy Powell.' The first inside page is also engraved in gold letters with the words, 'This book is presented to Sandy Powell as a memento of his appearance as the subject of "This is Your Life".' This is followed with a hand-written message: 'All of us were honoured to have had the chance to pay our small tribute to a great laughter-maker. Eamon Andrews.' The other pages are filled with photographs both in colour and black and white, of all those that took part in the programme, with appropriately worded captions on each. Attached to the inside back cover is a pocket containing a double-sided gramophone record, a complete transcription of every word spoken in the memorable programme. It is a volume that Sandy will cherish for the rest of his life. His one regret is that, deleted from the screen show, perhaps because of lack of time, were the two men who did so much towards its making, Norman Meadows and Arthur Lane, without whose help things may have not run so smoothly nor turned out so successfully.

Sandy's Golden Year of 1970 had a happy finish when Kay and he flew out to South Africa to tour with the show so aptly named *The Golden Years of Music Hall*.

II

Away from Home

SANDY first toured South Africa in 1929 when accompanied by his wife Peggy. They sailed the six thousand miles on the liner *Edinburgh Castle* to Cape Town. It was of course long before the days of air travel, and Sandy says that, although it was much slower, it was far more pleasant, almost a holiday in itself. After an overnight stay at the Cape they went on by train, a journey of eight hundred miles to Johannesburg, where he was to play the Empire in a variety show as the second top of the bill. The star was 'Terpsicore', a dancer of international fame, whose speciality was dancing on the points of her toes. Sandy did two spots, a burlesque of 'Robinson Crusoe' in which he was assisted by Peggy, and also a single act, a monologue entitled 'The Boxer'. Engaged to play two weeks, Sandy made such a hit that they held him over for a further two weeks. The bill was changed and the British Lightweight Champion, Harry Mason, who was tremendously popular in South Africa, was top of the bill, doing shadow-boxing and sparring with a partner. He also played the violin, but Sandy says that Mason's violin-playing was as good as Sandy's boxing – 'ruddy awful!'

Also on the bill were Carlos Ames the famous harpist, the pantomimic absurdities of 'The Hanlon Brothers' and a popular act from Scotland 'Loch and Lomand.' Sandy was second top to the Hanlon Brothers at Benoni and then went on to Durban where he played for two weeks at the Criterion in a cine-variety show. This was followed by three weeks in Johannesburg at the Orpheum Cinema, where they featured three acts and films and finally a return to Cape Town for a month in variety at the Tivoli. His success there brought a demand for an extra week to play in cine-variety at the nearby town of Parle. His trip was most successful and most of the press reports of his show made it clear that he would be given a great welcome whenever he returned. As things turned out, his career in England was so successful he did not get a chance to go back as soon as he had hoped. In fact it was almost forty years later when at the end of 1970 he returned with *The Golden Years of Music Hall* company and found that they still remembered him.

This time the journey was not the leisurely, pleasant trip by ship, but by air, a means of transport that Sandy detests. He says that he'd sooner walk than fly, however far. A three months' tour had been arranged by impresario Arthur Lane, who also made an excellent Chairman for this great *Old Tyme Music Hall Show*. The cast was very strong: Sandy and Kay Powell, Walter Landauer (remaining partner of the world famous piano duo Rawitz and Landauer) Leslie Sarony, Maryetta Midgley (the singing daughter of the famous Covent Garden operatic tenor Walter Midgley), the great chorus singer Margery Manners and accordionists Reed and Delroy. They flew direct to Durban where their reception was almost overwhelming. When they got to their hotel, The Blue Waters, they found that the management had decorated the front of the hotel with a huge banner with a welcome greeting. It was the same at the Lyric cinema where their original three-week booking had to be extended for a further two weeks. The Lyric cinema, like so many in South Africa, was used for all kinds of shows.

Bill Brewer eminent stage and screen critic, in a review of the show at the Lyric Theatre, wrote:

The important words of the typically grandiose title 'The Golden Years of Music Hall' were, to me – 'Music Hall', because those two words conjured up a part of my life, a part that was warm, vibrant and unique. It was with a strange mixture of happy anticipation and trepidation that I awaited the going-up of the Lyric curtain on Sandy Powell, Leslie Sarony *et al.* – and their 'Golden Years of Music Hall'. I needn't have worried, all the artists on the generous bill stride the stage with authority. They all know their jobs, they are all experts, and their talents make for a laugh-filled happy evening that will make you remember it for years. Sandy Powell, when he reaches his ventriloquist bit, provides comedy that is as classic in its way as Charlie Chaplin's unforgettable dinner scene in 'The Gold Rush'. I laughed until my ribs ached and my eyes watered.

While in Durban, the company was asked to do a special matinee show for Indians and Pakistanis at a large Odeon cinema about ten miles outside Durban. It was packed to the doors, standing room only. The show went with a real swing, that is until just before the finale, when Sandy cracked a gag, an old music-hall favourite, which was always good for a laugh. He said, 'If you have enjoyed the show, please tell your friends, if not please keep your mouth shut. Please leave the theatre as quickly as possible because it is my turn to do the sweeping up.' Before he could continue, the packed audience, got up and started to walk out and by the time the finale got going the theatre was nearly empty.

Pinewood Cinema in Capetown was the next stop. It really was just a cinema. There were no proper dressing-room facilities and there were only three rooms altogether. Arthur Lane, with whom Sandy usually shared a dressing-room on tour, noticed some large lock-up garages at the side of the building and he persuaded the management to fit up one of them for Sandy and himself. They did a super job, decorated, carpeted and furnished the place with settees and armchairs, and installed a radio and electric fans. This sort of friendliness and hospitality was typical of how the company was met everywhere they worked. When they entered their hotel rooms on the first day, whether in the large or smaller towns, the first thing they saw were the flowers and a bottle of champagne. The audiences were enthusiastic and business tremendous; in fact the tour had to be extended for a further two months.

The point of final departure was the airport at Johannesburg where security was stringent and luggage was searched before being allowed to go on the plane. In Sandy's baggage was a large cavalry-type sword which he used in the vent act. A rather serious security officer proceeded to make an issue of it. The matter was settled by the pilot taking the sword in the cockpit and returning it to Sandy later on. Sandy, Kay, Arthur and Audrey did not go back with the rest of the company; the tour had been pretty strenuous and they decided to break the journey at Las Palmas in the Canary Islands and stop over for a few days' rest. At the airport coming home Sandy was again concerned in an encounter with an official. Examining the passport he asked, 'How did you get into Las Palmas, there is no entry stamp?' Calling over a higher official, and then another, they held quite a conference over Sandy's passport, with him getting more and more agitated with the thought of having to spend the rest of his days in a Spanish jail. That Sandy's Spanish was far worse than their English didn't help matters. Eventually somebody noticed a faint trace of a rubber stamp on one of the pages, and a much relieved Sandy was allowed to board the plane for home.

During 1973 there was talk about the company doing an even more ambitious tour of South Africa and New Zealand, soon after the finish of their summer season at Brighton. The company included Sandy, Elsie and Doris Waters, Cavan O'Connor, Bob and Alf Pearson, Margery Manners, and Don Smoothey. There were many hold-ups in the arrangements; first it was on and then it was off. Time went by and it looked very much as if it wasn't going to happen. Sandy's old friend Alan Gale kept on nagging him to join his pantomime to be held at Tunbridge Wells. There was a good part in it for Kay, too, and as it was not far from home, Sandy signed the contract. Not long after he did this a message came through from Arthur Lane to say that the tour was on and that they were leaving in mid December. He suggested that Sandy and Kay join them in South Africa in January 1974 and then go on with the company to New Zealand.

So Sandy and Kay found themselves flying to Cape Town after the pantomime season and being met at the airport by Audrey Lupton just after midnight. Audrey said, 'We are going straight to the theatre where Arthur is throwing a party after the show.' It was nearly one o'clock in the morning by the time they got there and Audrey took them to a large tea room. When she opened the door they saw that it was a candle-light welcome party. It was a very well-intentioned gesture, but they obviously did not realise that Sandy and Kay had just travelled six thousand miles from England where, due to power cuts, candle-lit rooms were the order of the day. They said nothing and enjoyed the fun. 'Black Velvet Candlelight

Parties' were all the rage in South Africa at that time; they had just been introduced to the new gimmick, mixing champagne with Guiness beer, a concoction nicknamed 'Black Velvet'.

The company was working at the Hoffmeir Theatre and, by special request, Sandy appeared at their final performance there as 'Special Guest Artist'. The company moved on the next day to Port Elizabeth while Kay and Sandy stayed on for a well-earned holiday. At a minute past midnight on 30th January, the telephone rang in the bedroom and the operator said that there was a personal call for Mr Sandy Powell from Port Elizabeth. It was every member of the company wishing him a happy birthday – his

A million-to-one chance meeting in Christchurch, New Zealand in 1974 between Sandy and the captain of the rugby team that toured England in 1947, Pat Smith.

seventy-fourth. This was typical of the friendly spirit and comradeship of these grand pros. The company finished their tour at Johannesburg and Sandy and Kay travelled there to join up with the party a few days before all leaving together for New Zealand. On the plane Sandy said to Arthur Lane, 'I think I'll drop my opening line "Can you hear me Mother?". Nobody in New Zealand will know anything about it.' Arthur advised him to leave the matter open until they got there. Val Doonican was on the plane and when they landed at Auckland they were both whisked off to do television interviews.

The next morning they went to the theatre for band call. Arthur Lane recalls: 'Sandy and I walked to the theatre down one of the main streets and an old lady stopped us and said "Ee, it's Sandy Powell". Passers-by, hearing her remark, stopped us as we moved on, and soon people were calling out "Can you hear me Mother?" and Sandy was nearly mobbed. This was the man who said nobody would know him in New Zealand. Younger people were also wanting to speak to him, and this made me curious, and enquiring around I discovered that he was the best known of our company, because his old seventy-eight records were being played regularly on the radio both in Australia and New Zealand. In fact in Auckland and when touring the country, when Sandy was on stage, members of the audience called out: 'What about doing "Sandy the Policeman" or "Sandy the Dentist".' Sandy used to tell them, 'I wish I could remember them. I made them forty years ago.'

It was in this sort of atmosphere that they opened at Her Majesty's Theatre. So it was no wonder when Sandy stepped out on to the stage at the first performance and spoke his opening line, 'Can you hear me Mother?', he got a fantastic reception and every gag he cracked from then on got a big round of applause. It gave a great start to the show. But a strange thing happened in the second half. Sandy did his classic sketch 'The Ventriloquist'. Sandy says: 'Normally it never misses. But there it didn't get a titter, not a sausage.' Sandy could not understand it. He thought, 'I've flown all these thousands of miles to flop with one of my biggest certainties.' He stuck it out for a week but it never registered so instead he decided to do his conjurer's burlesque. It was a big hit! Every performance was a sell-out and the same thing happened at all the other theatres played in Hamilton, Wanganui and Palmerston North. It was all go but most enjoyable. Nevertheless they were glad to get to their last date on North Island, at Wellington where their extended stay gave them a chance to get their breath back.

On this tour, they not only played the theatres, but the company was also in great demand for TV and radio interviews. Radio was particularly important there; practically every town had a local radio station from which they did interview, chat or record sessions. Listeners would be invited to telephone in with requests for Sandy to play their favourite records. Sandy sometimes talked to the men and Margery Manners to the women, or vice-versa. One programme that impressed Sandy and Kay was called *Lost and Found*, in which callers would tell of articles lost or found. Another was a

Swappit programme; callers would offer to swap items. 'Anything you can't get, we'll get for you,' was a feature in this show. Kay was on the air one day and mentioned that she had run out of Sparklet bulbs for her soda-water-making bottle. Within a few minutes a shopkeeper telephoned to say that if she called at a particular address, he would be pleased to let her have them. On one of the record-request programmes that Sandy did, the callers contributed a sum of money to a specified local charity to have their requests answered. One man rang to say that he was a Yorkshireman, and he would give a couple of pounds if Sandy would sing, 'On Ilkley Moor Bar Tat'. Almost immediately another man rang to say that he had originally come from Lancashire, and that he'd give a fiver if Sandy did not! The second offer was accepted.

Arthur Lane had an interesting message of good will to take to a town a few miles from Wellington – a town called Eastbourne which was linked as a sister town with Eastbourne in England. The company was given a great welcome there and were conducted through their beautiful town hall and saw the handsome mayoral chair which was presented by the Eastbourne (England) Corporation to· the Eastbourne, (New Zealand) Corporation as a token of thanks for the food parcels sent to England during the 1939–45 War.

They next flew to the beautiful city of Christchurch on the South Island. That night Sandy and Kay, having a fancy for a Chinese meal, found a restaurant, but they did not have a licence to serve drinks and the proprietor recommended they visit the public house next door. When they entered the pub it caused quite a stir when a young man went up to them and said, 'I'd like to show you something.' It was a photograph hanging on the wall, a picture taken in 1947 of a group of New Zealand rugby players with Sandy in his dressing-room at the Empire, Leeds! Pointing to a man in the photograph the young man said, 'That's my father, Pat Smith, he was the captain of that touring side. I know that he would be thrilled to see you.' They quickly found him, and marvelled at the extraordinary coincidence that on the very first night of their arrival, they had, out of the thousands of places they could have gone into, been directed to this pub, to see a photograph proudly displayed on the wall, a picture taken forty years before of Sandy and the proprietor.

Invercargill, the nearest town to the South Pole was the next date, to be followed by Dunedin for the next booking. But on arrival Arthur saw that every seat had been sold for the three days' and it was obvious they could have done with more time there. An extra performance was hurriedly arranged, and a full house resulted.

Dunedin gave them a great reception and it was with reluctance that they left there for a long flight to Auckland, and then an even longer one back to England. It had been another highly successful trip and Arthur had tempting offers to return the following year to both South Africa and New Zealand, and also Australia. Frankly Sandy and the company could stay over there for a year at least touring those countries and at the end of the